Are you interested in

a course management system that would

save you time & effort?

If the answer is *yes*, **CourseCompass is for you.**

Contact your local Allyn & Bacon/Longman sales representative for a free access code, or visit www.coursecompass.com, and take a tour of this course management system.

Technical support is available for faculty and students:
support@coursecompass.com
1-800-677-6337

CourseCompass is an online course management system designed to help you manage all the aspects of your course — communication, information distribution, testing and grading.

Let it help you:

- **Communicate directly with your students** via email, discussion boards, and announcement pages.
- **Post documents for your course,** eliminating the need for course packs or handouts.
- **Administer online tests,** with automatic grading and analysis.
- **Provide your students with 24/7 access** to key course information, such as syllabus, assignments, and additional resources – as well as check his/her grade instantly.

Demo CourseCompass today! www.coursecompass.com

THE IRIS CENTER
FOR FACULTY ENHANCEMENT
Peabody College at Vanderbilt University

Enhance your course with these *free* online resources from IRIS!

WHAT IS IRIS?
The IRIS Center for Faculty Enhancement is based at Vanderbilt University's Peabody College and supported through a federal grant. The goal of the IRIS Center is to create course enhancement materials for college faculty who teach pre-service general education teachers, school administrators, school counselors and school nurses.

WHAT RESOURCES DOES IRIS HAVE?
IRIS course enhancement materials are designed to better prepare school personnel to provide an appropriate education to students with disabilities. To achieve this goal, IRIS has created free course enhancement materials for college faculty in the following areas:

• Accommodations • Behavior • Collaboration • Disability • Diversity • Instruction

These resources include online interactive modules, case study units, information briefs, student activities, an online dictionary, and a searchable directory of disability-related web sites. These resource materials are designed for use as supplements to college classes (e.g., homework assignments) or as in-class activities.

STAR LEGACY MODULES
Challenge-based interactive lessons are provided using *STAR Legacy* modules. The following is a list of some of the many modules available on the IRIS website:
- A Clear View: Setting Up Your Classroom for Students with Visual Disabilities
- Who's in Charge? Developing a Comprehensive Behavior Management System
- You're in Charge! Developing A Comprehensive Behavior Management Plan
- Addressing the Revolving Door: How to Retain Your Special Education Teachers
- What Do You See? Perceptions of Disability
- Teachers at the Loom: Culturally and Linguistically Diverse Exceptional Students
- See Jane Read: Teaching Reading to Young Children of Varying Disabilities

CASE STUDIES
IRIS case studies include three levels of cases for a given topic, with each level requiring higher-level analysis and understanding from students.
- Fostering Student Accountability For Classroom Work
- Effective Room Arrangement
- Early Reading
- Norms and Expectations
- Encouraging Appropriate Behavior
- Reading: Word Identification/Fluency, Grades 3-5
- Reading: Comprehension/Vocabulary, Grades 3-5

WEB RESOURCE DIRECTORY
These online directories help faculty members and college students to search by category to find information about websites on the special education or disability topic of their interest.

All IRIS materials are available to faculty at no cost through the IRIS website http://iris.peabody.vanderbilt.edu or on CD by request to the IRIS Center (1-866-626-IRIS).

Instructor's Manual

for

Best and Kahn

Research in Education

Tenth Edition

prepared by

James V. Kahn
University of Illinois at Chicago

Boston   New York   San Francisco
Mexico City   Montreal   Toronto   London   Madrid   Munich   Paris
Hong Kong   Singapore   Tokyo   Cape Town   Sydney

Copyright © 2006 Pearson Education, Inc.

All rights reserved. The contents, or parts thereof, may be reproduced with *Research in Education*, Tenth Edition, by John W. Best and James V. Kahn, provided such reproductions bear copyright notice, but may not be reproduced in any form for any other purpose without written permission from the copyright owner.

To obtain permission(s) to use the material from this work, please submit a written request to Allyn and Bacon, Permissions Department, 75 Arlington Street, Boston, MA 02116 or fax your request to 617-848-7320.

ISBN 0-205-47819-0

Printed in the United States of America

10 9 8 7 6 5 4 3 2 1   09 08 07 06 05

TABLE OF CONTENTS

CHAPTER 1:	THE MEANING OF RESEARCH	1
CHAPTER 2:	SELECTING A PROBLEM AND PREPARING A RESEARCH PROPOSAL.	7
CHAPTER 3:	THE RESEARCH REPORT	13
CHAPTER 4:	HISTORICAL RESEARCH	20
CHAPTER 5:	DESCRIPTIVE STUDIES: ASSESSMENT, EVALUATION, AND RESEARCH	25
CHAPTER 6:	EXPERIMENTAL AND QUASI-EXPERIMENTAL RESEARCH	30
CHAPTER 7:	SINGLE-SUBJECT EXPERIMENTAL RESEARCH	38
CHAPTER 8:	QUALITATIVE RESEARCH	43
CHAPTER 9:	METHODS AND TOOLS OF RESEARCH	47
CHAPTER 10:	DESCRIPTIVE DATA ANALYSIS	55
CHAPTER 11:	INFERENTIAL DATA ANALYSIS	66
CHAPTER 12:	COMPUTER DATA ANALYSIS	76

PREFACE

This instructor's manual is the sixth for *Research in Education*. Many instructors desire a manual consisting primarily of test questions. Thus, I have written a number of test items for each chapter in the text. The items cover material retained from the previous editions as well as the new material that I have added to the text. The number of items provided for each chapter varies according to the length and content of the chapter. This manual differs from the previous ones in that it also includes overhead masters for most of the Tables, Figures and Appendices.

Although most instructors will probably only administer midterm and final exams, this manual provides items for each chapter so that an instructor may give tests on individual chapters or on certain discrete chapters. The questions for each chapter do not rely upon information or language from any other chapter. Thus, instructors who use the chapters of the text in a different order or who do not cover certain chapters may still use the test items without concern.

There is some overlap of content among chapters and, therefore, among test items from different chapters. Instructors should read through their exams to make sure that there are not two questions on very similar content or that one question does not suggest an answer for another question. Random ordering of test questions once they are selected provides a better test of the material.

The book was written primarily for use as a text in an introductory course on research methods and statistics. It may also serve as a reference book for students writing a thesis or for those who wish to carry out a research study.

Some of the topics covered in the text may be peripheral to the course objectives of some instructors. It is not suggested that all of the topics in the book be included in a single course. It is recommended that instructors use the topics selectively and in the sequence that they find most appropriate. Unused portions of the book might then be used in a subsequent course (some universities have a two-course sequence), to assist the student in carrying out a thesis, or as a reference.

I wish to thank my wife, Kathleen Cuerdon-Kahn and my son Gabe for their encouragement and support throughout the entire project of revising the text as well as this test manual.

James V. Kahn

CHAPTER ONE

THE MEANING OF RESEARCH

Key Definitions and Concepts:

deductive reasoning	sampling error
inductive reasoning	simple random sampling
scientific approach	systematic sampling
theory	stratified random sampling
research hypothesis	area or cluster sampling
null hypothesis	replication
statistic	fundamental research
parameter	applied research
sample	action research
population	assessment
randomization	evaluation
random selection	descriptive research
scientific approach	historical research
characteristics of research	experimental research

Multiple-Choice Test Items

1. Which of the following characteristics distinguishes the research hypothesis
   from an informal hypothesis?
   In a research hypothesis
   a) multiple research outcomes should be predicted.
   *b) variables must be operationally defined.
   c) there are direct causal relationships being investigated.
   d) only one outcome is predicted.

2. Operationally defined variables
   a) are seldom manipulated by the experimenter.
   *b) describe behaviors which can be directly observed.
   c) are inconsistent with scientific method.
   d) are attribute variables.

3. The null hypothesis
   a) is rejected when an experimenter observes no effects due to his
      intervention.
   b) states that the sampling process must be random and representative.
   *c) asserts that observed differences are due to chance errors in the sampling
      process.
   d) asserts a causal link between two or more variables.

1

4. The ideal sample
    a) is not simply randomly selected.
    b) is concerned only with the experimental group.
  *c) is both representative and economical.
    d) never exceeds sixteen subjects.

5. Randomization ensures
    a) the selection of a sample group that is different than its population.
    b) rejection of the null hypothesis.
  *c) that the experimental and control groups are equated for the experiment.
    d) sample bias.

6. Sampling error
    a) refers to the mistakes made by an experimenter during the sampling
       process.
    b) cannot be accounted for by current data analysis techniques.
    c) is never reduced by randomization.
  *d) refers to the chance variations that occur in the sampling process.

7. Which of the following is not a feature of a simple random sample?
    a) Individual observations or individuals each have an equal chance of being
       selected.
    b) Each selection choice is independent of any other choice.
    c) The population from which the sample is drawn is defined.
  *d) All of these are important features of a simple random sample.

8. Systematic sampling
    a) requires an infinite or unknown population.
    b) allows us to reject the null hypothesis.
  *c) consists of the selection of each nth term from a list designating the
       population.
    d) leads to systematic bias.

9. In order to construct a stratified random sample, the experimenter:
  *a) subdivides the population into smaller homogeneous groups.
    b) randomly selects only a few of the smaller homogeneous groups of a
       given population.
    c) is not concerned with the representativeness of the sample.
    d) selects part of a simple random sample.

10. The area or cluster sample
    a) is likely to introduce sample bias because of the unequal size of the
       subsets selected.
    b) is used when the population is infinite.
    c) involves successive random sampling of geographic areas eventually
       selecting a sample of individuals.
  *d) all of the above.

11. A sample made up of volunteers may be biased because:
   a) the control group and the experimental group can never be equated.
   b) it is not economical.
  *c) they may not be representative of the total population.
   d) none of the above.

12. A sample is considered large if it includes no less than
   a) 10 individuals.
   b) 15 individuals.
   c) 25 individuals.
  *d) 30 individuals.

13. Sampling error decreases
  *a) as sample size increases.
   b) as sample size decreases.
   c) when volunteers are used.
   d) when random selection is eliminated.

14. Which of the following is not a characteristic of research?
   a) It is directed to the solution of a problem.
   b) It requires accurate observations and controls.
   c) It emphasizes the development of generalizations and principles that can
      be used for prediction of future occurrences.
  *d) It guarantees that personal bias will be eliminated.

15. Replication
   a) is concerned with randomization.
  *b) is concerned with the deliberate duplication of a study to confirm the
      conclusions of a previous study.
   c) involves using the same subjects for another experiment.
   d) none of the above.

16. Which characteristic is not representative of applied research?
   a) It is concerned with improving a product or process.
   b) It is often used in educational research.
  *c) It is usually carried out in a laboratory.
   d) It is concerned with testing theoretical concepts in actual problem
      situations.

17. Which of the following is not a characteristic of educational action
      research?
   a) It is focused on immediate application.
   b) Its findings should be evaluated in terms of local applicability.
   c) It involves both the research specialist and the classroom teachers.
  *d) Its findings usually have universal validity.

18. Assessment
   a) is concerned with hypothesis testing.
   b) is concerned with making recommendations.
   *c) is a fact-finding activity.
   d) none of the above.

19. Evaluation
   a) never involves recommendations.
   *b) is concerned with judgments as to the effectiveness and utility of
       programs.
   c) is concerned with findings that can be generalized to other settings.
   d) none of the above.

20. Descriptive research
   *a) is concerned with hypothesis formulation and testing.
   b) is concerned with manipulated variables.
   c) is seldom ex post facto.
   d) all of the above.

21. A type of research concerned with describing future events predicted by the
    manipulation of variables is
   a) historical research.
   b) descriptive research.
   *c) experimental research.
   d) all of the above.

22. Which statement is not a problem with research conducted with humans as
    subjects?
   a) People are not consistent in their behavior.
   b) People are not alike in feelings, drives, and emotions.
   c) People are influenced by the research process itself.
   *d) All of the above are Problems.

23. Which of the following is not an element of a syllogism?
   *a) Specific observations.
   b) Major premise.
   c) Minor premise.
   d) Conclusion.

24. The deductive method is best described as
   a) a self-evident assumption.
   *b) a method of reasoning which moves from the general assumption to the
       specific application.
   c) a method of reasoning which moves from specific observations
       to a generalization.
   d) a theory of logic.

25. The inductive method is best described as
  a) individual observations.
  b) a method of reasoning which moves from the general assumption to the specific application.
  *c) a method of reasoning which moves from specific observations to a generalization.
  d) a theory of logic.

26. The deductive-inductive method is best described as
  a) a major collaborative effort of Aristotle and Francis Bacon.
  b) a method of reasoning which moves from the general assumption to the specific application.
  c) a method of reasoning which moves from specific observations to a generalization.
  *d) a method of reasoning in which a hypothesis is tested by the collection and logical analysis of data.

27. Which of the following statements about theory is not true?
  a) The development of theory is one of the primary functions of science.
  b) The scientist is engaged in the use, modification, and/or creation of theory.
  *c) Because human nature is so simplistic, it is easier to develop sound theories of human behavior than to predict occurrences in the physical world.
  d) The scientist begins with a set of ideas that direct the effort and with a goal that entails the development of testing of theory.

28. A theory
  a) establishes a cause and effect relationship between variables with the purpose of explaining and predicting phenomena.
  b) defines nonobservable constructs that are inferred from observable facts and events and that are thought to have an effect on the phenomenon under study.
  c) describes the relationship among key variables for purposes of explaining a current state or predicting future occurrences.
  *d) all of the above.

29. A hypothesis
  a) is a theory.
  *b) can be used to test an existing theory.
  c) is not used to develop a theory.
  d) is never rejected based upon research findings.

Essay Test Items and Topics for Class Discussion:

1. What characteristics distinguish the research hypothesis from a personal hypothesis?

2. Why is it important that the experimenter be able to reject the null hypothesis?

3. What distinguishes a statistic from a parameter?

4. Describe two important applications that randomization has concerning research?

5. Why must the experimenter be concerned with sampling error?

6. Why is it important for the experimenter to be able to define the population of research interest?

7. How would you go about obtaining a stratified random sample concerning a survey of all school-age children in your city?

8. How would you go about obtaining an area or cluster sample concerning a survey of all church organizations in the United States in order to get information concerning individual members' attitudes toward human rights struggles around the world?

9. Why does the use of volunteers as subjects in an experiment create possibility of a biased sample?

10. Describe several important characteristics of scientific research.

11. Describe how assessment differs from evaluation.

12. What are the distinguishing characteristics of fundamental, applied and action research

13. What are the major differences between descriptive and experimental research?

CHAPTER 2

SELECTING A PROBLEM AND PREPARING A RESEARCH PROPOSAL

Key Definitions and Concepts:

the academic research project
levels of research projects
sources of research problems
evaluation of the research problem
the research proposal
statement of the problem
definitions
assumptions
limitations
delimitations
the review of related literature
the hypothesis
the method section
proposals

the subject section
the procedure section
time schedules
experimental ethics
informed consent
invasion of privacy
confidentiality
finding related literature
note-taking guidelines
references
bibliography
the first research report
seeking funding for research

Multiple-Choice Test Items:

1. The reason selecting a research problem is so difficult for the beginning
researcher is that
   a. the beginning researcher is likely to select a problem that is too broad in
scope.
   b. the beginning researcher is usually naive about related research literature.
   c. his or her research activity may be fragmentary and bear little relevance to
the formulation of theory.
   *d. all of the above.

2. Research is
   a. a process of proving theories.
   *b. a process of testing hypotheses.
   c. a subjective, individual process.
   d. all of the above.

3. Invasion of privacy
   a. is concerned with generalizing publicly recorded behaviors.
   b. suggests that public behavior cannot be observed ethically.
   *c. is concerned about the use of private correspondence without the subject's
knowledge and permission.
   d. all of the above.

7

4. Informed consent
   a. is not necessary when subjects are mentally incapacitated.
   b. is not necessary when the subjects are minors.
  *c. includes the freedom to withdraw from an experiment without reprisal.
   d. all of the above.

5. The research hypothesis
   a. may be formulated after the data are gathered.
   b. need not be consistent with known facts or theories.
  *c. should be stated in such a way that it can be tested and found to be
        probably true or probably false.
   d. all of the above.

6. Additional hypotheses formulated after data are collected
   a. are always inappropriate.
   b. are necessary for an unbiased investigation.
   c. should be included in the review of the literature.
  *d. should be tested on the basis of new data.

7. Which is not a function of the Procedure section in a research proposal?
   a. It describes in detail what is to be done in the experiment.
   b. It describes in detail what data-gathering devices will be used.
  *c. It describes in detail who the subjects will be.
   d. It describes in detail what data will be needed.

8. The limitations of the beginning researcher
   a. imply that the results of his or her research will be unimportant.
  *b. put the emphasis on learning how to conduct research.
   c. should be no different than those researchers pursuing doctoral
        dissertations.
   d. prevent him or her from expanding the first research problem into a more
        comprehensive treatment at a later date.

9. In a research proposal the statement of the problem
   a. presents broad areas of concern from which many problems are presented.
   b. does not suggest a specific definitive solution.
  *c. must be limited in scope to make a definite conclusion.
   d. must not be based on personal observation or experience.

10. Assumptions
   a. are criteria used to define observable samples of behavior.
  *b. are statements of belief that a researcher cannot verify.
   c. are the boundaries of that particular study.
   d. are never presented in the research proposal.

11. In a research proposal, limitations are
    a. the boundaries of that particular study.
    b. independent variables expressed in operational terms.
    *c. conditions beyond the researcher's control that may restrict the conclusions of the study.
    d. all of the above.

12. In a research proposal, delimitations are
    *a. the boundaries of that particular study.
    b. independent variables expressed in operational terms.
    c. conditions beyond the researcher's control that may restrict the conclusions from the study.
    d. all of the above.

13. In a research proposal, the review of related literature
    a. includes a long list of annotated studies that relate to the problem.
    b. includes poorly executed studies as well as competent ones.
    *c. signifies the researcher is familiar with what is already known and what remains untested.
    d. all of the above.

14. Research makes its contribution to human welfare by
    a. supplying quick and fairly spectacular solutions to social problems.
    *b. countless small additions of knowledge.
    c. selecting problems that are very broad in scope.
    d. proving existing theories.

15. Which of the following is a likely source to which one may go for a suitable research problem?
    a. Problems confronted in the classroom or school.
    b. Technological changes that are currently happening.
    c. Consultation with an advisor or professor.
    *d. All of the above.

16. Which question would be considered last when initially evaluating a research problem?
    a. Is the problem significant?
    b. Are pertinent data accessible?
    c. Am I competent enough to plan and carry out a study of this type?
    *d. How will it be funded?

17. The statement of the problem is inappropriate when
    a. it is written in question form.
    b. its major statement is followed by minor statements.
    c. it is not derived from personal observation and experience.
    *d. it does not allow for specific answers.

18. Significance of the problem refers to
    a. the distinguishing and unusual terms of a study that could be misinterpreted.
    *b. justifying its worth for conducting a study.
    c. the number of variables that can be considered in operational terms.
    d. the boundaries of the research Problem.

19. A data-gathering device that has not been validated is an example of
    a. a definition.
    b. an assumption.
    *c. a limitation.
    d. a delimitation.

20. A researcher's insistence that after three days observers will not have a reactive effect on subjects' behavior is an example of
    a. a definition.
    *b. an assumption.
    c. a limitation.
    d. a delimitation.

21. A study of addition performance concerned only with learning disabled students is an example of
    a. a definition.
    b. an assumption.
    c. a limitation.
    *d. a delimitation.

22. In searching for related literature, the researcher should take note of
    a. faults that could have been avoided.
    b. reports of studies of closely related problems previously investigated.
    c. the design of the study and the populations that were sampled.
    *d. all of the above.

23. Time schedules are important because
    a. they include a detailed outline about how the research will be carried out.
    *b. they help to systematize the study and avoid procrastination.
    c. they outline the frequencies of variables used in the study.
    d. all of the above.

24. Observing and recording public behavior of anonymous persons
    a. is still an invasion of privacy.
    *b. is not an invasion of privacy.
    c. still requires informed consent.
    d. both b and c.

25. A standard score on an achievement test would most likely be used as an operational definition for
a. creativity.
*b. knowledge.
c. coordination.
d. self-esteem.

26. "There will be no differences in reading comprehension gains of learning disabled students in the fourth grade due to a direct instruction method as compared to a group of normal peers."
This is an example of
a. a research hypothesis.
*b. a null hypothesis.
c. an operational definition.
d. a research assumption.

Essay Test Items and Topics for Class Discussion:

1. Why is selecting a research proposal such a difficult problem for the novice?

2. Select a research problem and try to narrow its scope so that a study could be proposed from it.

3. What can be done to encourage students who have received training in research activities to carry out studies on their own?

4. What obstacles must a part-time student overcome concerning conducting research that may not apply to the full-time student.

5. Review and discuss the many sources to which the beginning researcher may go for a suitable research problem.

6. From the list of sixty problem sources suggested by the text, select some of interest and practice narrowing the scope of the research problem.

7. Discuss four important questions which a researcher must consider before a proposed research problem can be deemed appropriate.

8. Review and discuss the importance of the ten guidelines suggested by the text when taking notes for the research Proposal.

9. Review and discuss the twelve suggestions presented in the text concerning those who may want to seek financial support for their research proposal.

10. Why is it necessary to indicate how your study will add to or refine present knowledge?

11. Why must a research proposal possess the qualities of significance, originality and feasibility?

12. Review and discuss the important elements that the researcher should note when searching for related literature of the research problem.

13. Why are time schedules useful?

14. What are the major areas of concern that a researcher must review when regarding ethics in human experimentation?

CHAPTER 3

THE RESEARCH REPORT

<u>Key Definitions and Concepts:</u>

the research report
style manuals
format of the research report:
  title page
  abstract
  method section
  results section
  discussion section
  references
  appendices
the dissertation
writing styles

typographical standards for
  the dissertation
reference forms
pagination
tables
figures
line graphs
bar graphs
circle or sector charts
maps
organization charts
evaluation of a research report

<u>Multiple-Choice Test Items:</u>

1. Which is not a characteristic of the abstract in a research report?
  a. It includes the characteristics of the subjects.
  b. It includes the findings of the study.
  c. It includes the conclusions reached by the researcher.
*d. It includes a short review of the literature.

2. Which is not a component of a well-written introduction appearing in the
    research report?
  a. A clear and definitive statement of the problem.
  b. A review of previous literature on the topic.
  c. Formal statements for each hypothesis presented.
*d. A detailed description of the procedures that are used in the study.

3. Which is not a component of the method section in a research report?
  a. It includes at least two subsections, one describing subjects and the other
    procedures.
  b. It is sufficiently detailed so as to be replicable.
  c. It describes measurement devices, the experimental group and the
    assignment of subjects to conditions.
*d. It includes the data analyses.

4. Which is not in the results section in a research report?
  a. It presents the data and statistical analyses.
*b. It includes all relevant findings except those which do not support the
    hypotheses.
  c. It includes no discussion of the implications of the findings.
  d. none of the above are in the results section.

13

5. Which is not a characteristic of the discussion section of a research report?
   a. It is presented as the final section.
   b. It determines the implications of the study including whether the hypotheses were supported or should be rejected.
   *c. All relevant findings are presented including those that do not support the hypotheses of the investigator.
   d. It includes a brief discussion of the limitations of the present investigation.

6. Tables do not
   a. enable the reader to comprehend and interpret data rapidly.
   b. include summaries of statistical analyses.
   c. ever exceed the page size of the manuscript.
   *d. Tables do all of the above.

7. Which is not a characteristic of figures used in a research report?
   a. They are used to present statistical data in graphic form.
   b. They include a wide variety of graphs, charts, maps and diagrams.
   *c. They are used as substitutes for textual descriptions.
   d. None of the above are characteristic of figures.

8. Which of the following sections of a research report includes a review of the literature?
   a. The abstract.
   b. The discussion section.
   *c. The introduction.
   d. The method section.

9. Which of the following sections of a research report describes the study in 100-150 words?
   a. The introduction.
   *b. The abstract.
   c. The discussion section.
   d. The procedures section.

10. Which of the following sections of a research report includes a formal statement of each hypothesis?
   *a. The introduction.
   b. The discussion section.
   c. The results section.
   d. The method section.

11. Which of the following sections of a research report describes the actual steps carried out in conducting the study?
   a. The results section.
   *b. The procedures section.
   c. The discussion section.
   d. The introduction.

12. Which of the following sections of a research report presents the data and the statistical analyses?
a. The procedures section.
b. The discussion section.
c. The method section.
*d. The results section.

13. Which of the following sections of a research report includes proposals for future research?
a. The results section.
*b. The discussion section.
c. The method section.
d The introduction.

14. Which of the following sections of a research report is most likely to increase the readership of the article since so many persons start their reviews with this?
a. The introduction.
*b. The abstract.
c. The method section.
d. The discussion section.

15. Which of the following sections of a research report includes a definitive statement of the problem?
a. The procedures section.
b. The method section.
c. The discussion section.
*d. The introduction

16. Which of the following sections of a research report includes conclusions that reflect whether the original problem is better understood or even resolved as a result of the study?
a. The results section.
b. The introduction.
*c. The discussion section.
d. The method section

17. Which of the following types of data organization schemes shows the division of the unit into its component parts?
a. The bar graph.
*b. The sector chart.
c. The line graph.
d. The organization chart.

18. Which of the following data organization schemes illustrates the flow of authority, supervision or movement of materials from top to bottom?
a. The bar graph.
b. The sector chart.
c. The line graph.
*d. The organization chart.

19. Which of the following data organization schemes illustrates comparisons at different times by vertical columns?
*a. The bar graph.
b. The sector chart.
c. The line graph.
d. The organization chart.

20. Which of the following data organization schemes is useful in showing changes in data relationships over a period of time?
*a. The line graph.
b. The sector chart.
c. The bar graph.
d. The organization chart.

21. In the reference section, when no author is listed,
a. it is not necessary to cite an entry that is a research report.
b. it is not necessary to cite an entry that is a book.
*c. the first word of the title or sponsoring organization begins the entry.
d. it is not to be cited

22. Which of the following materials can generally be found in the appendices of research reports?
a. Unpublished tests.
b. Lengthy treatments not available elsewhere.
c. A new computer program.
*d. All of the above.

23. Which of the following statements is incorrect?
a. A goal of the thesis or dissertation is to demonstrate the author's knowledge in a particular field.
*b. In a dissertation, it is inappropriate to include raw data and computer printouts of the analyses performed.
c. The research report should describe and explain rather than try to convince or move persons to action.
d. All of the above are correct.

24. Which of the following elements are included in the research report?
a. A dedication line.
b. Standard statistical formulas.
*c. Any unusual formula used in the analysis.
d. All of the above are included.

25. Statistical symbols not available on the typewriter
   a. should be avoided.
   b. should be written with a pencil.
 *c. should be carefully inserted using black ink.
   d. should be footnoted.

Essay Test Items and Topics for Homework Assignments:

1. Write a critical analysis of the research report distributed (by the course instructor). Use the format suggested by the text to determine the quality of the various Darts of the report.

2. Determine the appropriate sort of figure to use and create one for the following situation. A researcher has counted the number of acting out behaviors of a child prior to, during, and after the intervention. The child acted out the following number of times on each day:

Prior to Intervention		During Intervention		After Intervention	
Day 1	15	Day 4	14	Day 8	2
Day 2	14	Day 5	10	Day 9	3
Day 3	12	Day 6	6	Day 10	1
		Day 7	2		

Answer Question 2: Line graph

3. Determine the appropriate sort of figure to use and create one for the following mythical data. Persons of both sexes are waiting until they are older to have their first child.

Average Males Ages	23	26	28
Average Female Ages	21	24	26

Answer Question 3: Bar Graph

4. Write the correct form for the following common reference types, given the information provided.

a. Book:
   Author: Jane Smith
   Title: Introduction to Psychology
   Publisher: Prentice-Hall, Inc.
   Copyright: 1984
   Place of publication: Englewood Cliffs, New Jersey

b. Chapter in Book:
   Author: John Lawless
   Chapter Title: Historical Research
   Book Title: Educational Research
   Editor: Lisa Mallow
   Publisher: Little, Brown and Company
   Place of publication: Boston, Massachusetts
   Copyright: In Press

c. Journal Article:
Authors: John Martin and Susan Ellis
Title: Friendship Patterns Among Mentally Retarded Adults
Journal: Mental Retardation
Copyright: 1984
Volume: 24
Pages: 27-43

Answers Question 4:

a. Smith, J. (1984). Introduction to psychology. Englewood Cliffs, NJ: Prentice-Hall.

b. Lawless, J. (in press). Historical research. In L. Mallow (Ed.), Educational research. Boston: Little, Brown.

c. Martin, J. & Ellis, S. (1981.). Friendship patterns among mentally retarded adults. Mental Retardation, 24, 27-43.

CHAPTER 4

HISTORICAL RESEARCH

<u>Key Definitions and Concepts:</u>

historical research
historical generalization
historical hypothesis
history and science
difficulties in historical research
primary sources of data
documents
hypotheses in educational historical
  research

relics
oral testimony
primary sources of educational data
secondary sources of data
external criticism
internal criticism
writing the historical report
criticism

<u>Multiple-Choice Test Items:</u>

1. Historical educational research differs from other types of research because
   a. we can safely make broad generalizations based on historical data.
   b. it does not require a review of the literature.
  *c. methods of observation are markedly different.
   d. historical research does not delimit the research problem.

2. Which of the following is not true of historical research?
   a. Objects of historical interest are not studied in isolation.
   b. Historical research is the application of the scientific method to the
      description and analysis of past events.
  *c. Historical research rigorously controls variables directly.
   d. Historical research depends upon accurate and objective observations of
      others.

3. Which is not an example of a primary source?
   a. Contracts between various people.
   b. Court decisions concerning past events.
   c. Film footage of a major event.
  *d. A discussion with a reporter who interviewed witnesses.

4. External criticism is concerned with
   a. the accuracy of historical evidence.
   b. the evaluation of a report by others in the field.
  *c. the authenticity of historical evidence.
   d. the extent to which we can generalize the findings.

5. Historical evidence
   a. can either be true or false.
   b. is validated more by external criticism.
   c. is more validated by internal criticism.
  *d. is a body of accepted valid information.

6. Valid historical research
   a. relies solely on primary sources.
   b. is unable to apply the scientific method to the description and analysis of past events.
   *c. confirms that few innovations in contemporary education are really new.
   d none of the above

7. A known forged document is an example of data that fails to pass the test of
   a. internal criticism.
   *b. external criticism.
   c. primary source significance.
   d. secondary source significance.

8. Which of the following is not a limitation exclusive to historical research?
   *a. The historian must delimit the problem and analyze primary data.
   b. The historian cannot safely generalize on the basis of past events.
   c. The historian must depend on the reported observations of others.
   d. None of the above.

9. Because it was difficult and costly to wage a war in Vietnam, one might predict that it would now be difficult and costly to wage a similar war in Iran. This is an example of a
   a. historical hypothesis.
   *b. historical generalization.
   c. historical criticism.
   d. historical documentation.

10. Which of the following primary sources of data is not "unconscious" testimony?
    a. Art objects.
    b. Clothing.
    *c. Wills.
    d. Weapons.

11. Which of the following statements is incorrect?
    *a. Objects of historical observation can be considered in isolation.
    b. Historians ordinarily draw their data from observation and experiences of others.
    c. A colorful, attractive, yet accurate style is permissible when doing historical research.
    d. All of the above are incorrect statements.

12. Historical criticism is the evaluation of
    *a. primary data.
    b. secondary data.
    c. historical hypotheses.
    d. a and b.
    e. all of the above.

13. Historical generalizations are
   a. impossible to establish.
  *b. established through a synthesis of compatible and incompatible evidence.
   c. only possible in trend studies.
   d. none of the above.

14. A criticism of historical research is that it does not
   a. delimit the research problem.
   b. employ the principles of probability.
   c. use hypotheses.
  *d. control the conditions of observations.

15. Historical hypotheses
   a. are always explicitly stated.
  *b. are confirmed when evidence is compatible.
   c. are not tested for significance.
   d. cannot be confirmed.

16. Which is not a difficulty exclusive to historical research?
   a. Contexts in which the events being studied occurred and were recorded must be considered.
   b. Researchers must depend upon inference and logical analyses, using the recorded experience of others.
   c. Appropriate primary sources of data must be found.
  *d. The research problem must be delimited.

17. Which of the following is not a primary source of educational data that might be useful in a historical research study?
   a. School newspapers.
   b. Attendance records.
  *c. A history of education textbook.
   d. A principal's diary.

18. Which of the following cannot be a document in a historical research study?
   a. Advertisements.
   b. Films.
   c. Licenses.
  *d. All of the above are documents.

19. Which of the following could most likely be considered both document and a relic?
   a. Food.
  *b. Pictures.
   c. Court decisions.
   d. Autobiographies.

20. Which of the following is not a characteristic of oral testimony?
   a. It is obtained in a personal interview.
   b. It is recorded or transcribed as the witness of an event relates his or her experience.
   *c. It is the spoken account of someone who spoke to a witness of an event.
   d. All of the above are characteristics of oral testimony.

21. Establishing the age or authorship of documents is a problem concerning
   a. internal criticism.
   *b. external criticism.
   c. problem delimitation.
   d. none of the above.

22. Establishing the accuracy or lack of bias of historical documents is a problem concerning
   *a. internal criticism.
   b. external criticism.
   c. problem delimitation.
   d. none of the above.

23. Which of the following is the least serious limitation of a historical study?
   a. Oversimplification.
   b. Overgeneralization.
   c. Failure to distinguish between significant and irrelevant facts in a situation.
   *d. Insufficient secondary sources of data.

24. According to proponents of historical research, which of the following is not a true statement?
   a. The historian cannot usually generalize on the basis of past events.
   b. Historians disagree on the validity of applying historical generalizations to different times and places.
   *c. The observations of historians are only reported in qualitative terms.
   d. Historians attempt to arrive at probability-type conclusions.

Essay Test Items and Topics for Class Discussion:

1. Discuss the limitations of historical research. Why are they limitations?

2. Critics of historical research distinguish historical research from scientific research activity. Discuss the characteristics that these critics use to distinguish these two types of research endeavors.

3. Proponents of historical research argue that historical research is more similar to than different from other forms of scientific research. Discuss the arguments used by the proponents.

4. Why is it so difficult for historical researchers to make generalizations from past events?

5. What is the difference between primary sources and secondary sources of data? Describe examples of primary and secondary sources of data that could be used in historical research concerned with secondary education in the 1860s.

6. Discuss the difficulties encountered in historical research and what must be done to limit their influence.

7. Describe some examples of documents, relics and oral testimony concerning contemporary primary or secondary education.

8. Describe some instances when a secondary source of data might also be used as a primary source of data.

9. Which is harder to determine - internal criticism or external criticism?

10. Describe several examples of easy-to-find secondary sources of data. What primary sources of data would improve the sources you have just selected?

CHAPTER 5

DESCRIPTIVE STUDIES: ASSESSMENT, EVALUATION, AND RESEARCH

<u>Key Definitions and Concepts:</u>

descriptive study
assessment
evaluation
social survey
ex post facto research
trend studies
replication

school surveys
follow-up studies
descriptive research
public opinion survey
activity analysis
secondary analysis
post hoc fallacy

<u>Multiple-Choice Test Items:</u>

1. Assessment
   a. is synonymous with evaluation.
   *b. describes a situation that prevails without value judgments.
   c. includes making recommendations for actions.
   d. is designed to determine the effectiveness of a particular program.

2. In descriptive research
   a. hypotheses are not tested.
   b. generalizations cannot be developed.
   *c. the researcher does not manipulate the variables under study.
   d. a and c.
   e. all of the above.

3. The differences among types of descriptive studies lie mostly in the
   a. nature of the conclusions.
   b. treatment of the data.
   c. motivation of the researcher.
   d. a and b.
   *e. all of the above.

4. The survey method is
   a. concerned with characteristics of individuals as individuals.
   b. not involved with a clearly defined problem and definite objectives.
   *c. concerned with gathering cross-sectional data.
   d. a and c.
   e. all of the above.

5. Activity analysis
   a. is based on longitudinal data.
   b. is not used for establishing job requirements.
   *c. is concerned with the processes that an individual is called upon for a given task.
   d. none of the above.

6. One inherent problem of *ex post facto* studies is that
   a. the researcher needs to arrange occurrences of the situation being studied.
   b. the researcher must live with the subjects under study for a long period of time.
   *c. information being sought may be incomplete.
   d. all of the above.

7. Secondary analysis refers to
   a. replicating a study using different subjects and settings.
   *b. reanalyzing data gathered by a previous investigator.
   c. the use of the same subjects for other related studies.
   d. none of the above.

8. Meta-analysis refers to
   *a. research synthesis that systematically and statistically combines the findings of previous studies.
   b. the combination of many hypotheses in a single study.
   c. studies involving more than a thousand subjects.
   d. statistical procedures that can eliminate the threat of the *post hoc* fallacy.

9. Which of the following is not a limitation of *ex post facto* research?
   a. The independent variable cannot be manipulated.
   b. Subjects cannot be randomly assigned to treatment groups.
   c. Causes are often multiple rather than single.
   *d. All of these are limitations.

10. Which of the following is not an assessment study?
    a. Surveys.
    b. Activity analysis.
    *c. Follow-up studies.
    d. Trend studies.

11. Which type of research would best describe the nature and extent of delinquency in large urban communities?
    a. A public opinion survey.
    *b. A social survey.
    c. An activity analysis.
    d. A follow-up study.

12. Which type of research would best obtain data for setting up an in-service program for improvement in job competence at a particular company?
   a. Trend analysis.
   *b. Activity analysis.
   c. Follow-up study.
   d. *Ex post facto* study.

13. To determine the impact that an institution's program had upon its students, a researcher would most likely conduct
   a. an *ex post facto* study.
   b. a trend study.
   c. an activity analysis.
   *d. a follow-up study.

14. Causal statements based upon *ex post facto* data are very difficult to make because
   a. of a lack of knowledge regarding what variables should be controlled and manipulated.
   b. it is impractical to arrange occurrences of behaviors and events.
   *c. of a lack of sufficient information about the events occurring at the time being studied.
   d. it is based upon a longitudinal consideration of data.

15. A researcher who incorrectly concludes that one factor is the cause and another is the effect, when, in fact, the two factors are only related,
   a. is committing an *ex post facto* fallacy.
   *b. is committing a *post hoc* fallacy.
   c. has used poor quota sampling techniques.
   d. has used poor probability sampling techniques.

16. Since there is a danger of confusing symptoms with causes, *ex post facto* researchers
   a. must employ quota sampling techniques.
   b. must carefully manipulate the independent variable.
   c. must randomly assign subjects to treatment groups.
   *d. none of the above.

17. Probability sampling
   a. is less accurate than quota sampling.
   *b. is more accurate than quota sampling.
   c. cannot be used in place of quota sampling.
   d. insures that the various components of the population are included in the same proportion they are represented in the population.

18. The fact that a new investigator may think of better hypotheses to be tested is an advantage of
   a. meta-analysis.
   *b. secondary analysis.
   c. replication studies.
   d. follow-up studies.
   e. All of the above.

19. An important method of challenging or verifying the conclusions of a previous study is known as
   a. meta-analysis.
   b. secondary analysis.
   *c. replication studies.
   d. follow-up studies.
   e. all of the above.

Essay Test Items and Topics for Class Discussion:

1. Select a local school problem and describe what people you would include in order to   conduct an evaluation of it. Defend your selections.

2. What educational problems or situations merit follow-up studies in order to evaluate their actual results? Defend your selections.

3. Why is it important for survey researchers to employ the appropriate sampling techniques with regard to the target population?

4. What improvements could result from activity analyses being conducted concerning industry and social agencies? Explain by example.

5. What social trends that you personally observe can be supported by existing data? How would you organize these data to support your claim?

6. What respondents should be included in a school survey concerning the imposition of a high school dress code? Defend your selections.

7. Describe some educational factors that may appear to have a cause-effect relationship yet result in a *post hoc* fallacy?

8. Why are scientists reluctant to state "cause and effect" conclusions from *ex Post facto* research data?

9. What data would you use to assess your students overall academic achievement gains? How would you justify the validity of the inclusion of each of these data?

10. Describe the differences and similarities that characterize assessment, evaluation and descriptive research.

11. Describe the differences and similarities that characterize social surveys, public opinion surveys and school surveys.

12. What problems inherent in *ex post facto* studies must the researcher be aware of and how can they be overcome?

13. What is the difference between replication and secondary analysis?

14. What is meant by the *post hoc* fallacy? Why is it a serious danger to *ex post facto* research?

15. What areas of education most warrant a national assessment?

16. Why is probability sampling preferred to quota sampling?

CHAPTER 6

EXPERIMENTAL AND QUASI-EXPERIMENTAL RESEARCH

Key Definitions and Concepts:

experimental group
control group
placebo
independent variable
dependent variable
confounding variable
intervening variable
extraneous variable
treatment variable
attribute variable
factorial designs
random assignment
sampling error
experimental variance
matched randomization
balancing cases (group matching)
analysis of covariance
operational definitions of variables
experimental validity
   internal validity and threats to it
   external validity and threats to it

blind
double blind
experimental designs
pre-experimental designs
static group comparison
one-shot case study
one group, pretest-posttest design
Hawthorne effect
main effect
true experimental designs
posttest only, equivalent groups design
pretest-posttest, equivalent groups design
Solomon four-group design
quasi-experimental designs
pretest-posttest, non-equivalent
groups design
time-series design
equivalent time-samples design
equivalent materials, pretest-posttest
   design
counterbalanced designs

Multiple-Choice Test Items:

1. In a true experiment
   a. the control group receives the treatment.
   *b. the control and experimental groups are randomly assigned.
   c. both control and experimental groups receive the treatment.
   d. it is not necessary to control for the Hawthorne effect.

2. The reactive effect of knowledge of participation in an experiment is known
   as
   a. the placebo effect.
   b. experimenter contamination.
   c. selection bias.
   *d. the Hawthorne effect.

3. A placebo control group can be distinguished from the more common control group
   a. because its subjects are volunteers.
   *b. because they receive a placebo and the more common control group receives nothing additional.
   c. because the common control group is randomly assigned.
   d. because members of a placebo control group are not equated to the experimental group previous to the experiment.

4. Which of the following statements concerning true experiments is not correct?
   a. True experiments are characterized by a treatment/non-treatment.
   b. Varying types or amounts of the experimental factor may be applied to number of groups.
   c. Subjects are randomly assigned to experimental or control groups.
   *d. The independent variable is not manipulated by the experimenter.

5. Treatment variables are those
   a. characteristics of the subjects that cannot be altered by the experimenter.
   *b. factors manipulated by the experimenter and to which subjects are assigned.
   c. characteristics that appear, disappear or change as the experimenter introduces, removes, or changes independent variables.
   d. characteristics of a study that influence the dependent variable and whose effect may be confused with the effect of the independent variable.

6. In an experiment, subjects' fatigue, anxiety and motivation while participating in a treatment are examples of
   a. extraneous variables.
   *b. intervening variables.
   c. selection bias.
   d. the Hawthorne effect.

7. Extraneous variables confound the results of a study when
   a. they are controlled for by the experimenter.
   b. they occur after the posttest.
   *c. they are correlated strongly enough with both the independent and dependent variables.
   d. all of the above.
   e. none of the above.

8. The influences of extraneous variables can be minimized by the use of
   a. random assignment.
   b. removing the variable from the study.
   c. analysis of covariance.
   *d. all of the above.

9. Matching cases
   a. is preferred to simple random assignment.
   *b. is used primarily in studies with a very small sample.
   c. eliminates the threat of experimenter bias.
   d. all of the above.

10. The most effective method of eliminating systematic bias and minimizing the effect of extraneous variables is provided by
   a. error variance.
   *b. random assignment.
   c. matching cases.
   d. none of the above.

11. Analysis of covariance
   a. is employed only with random assignment.
   b. cannot eliminate all initial differences on variables between experimental and control groups.
   *c. is considered preferable to the conventional matching of groups.
   d. is only used with a single independent variable.

12. Valid operational definitions must be
   a. based upon a theory that is generally recognized as valid.
   b. precise and stipulate the operations by which they could be observed.
   c. based upon relevant behaviors that can be observed and recorded.
   *d. all of the above.

13. Which is not a threat to internal validity?
   a. History.
   b. Maturation.
   *c. Interaction of selection and treatment.
   d. Statistical regression.

14. Which is not a threat to external validity?
   *a. Unstable instrumentation.
   b. Artificiality of the experimental setting.
   c. Interaction effect of testing.
   d. Interference of prior treatment.

15. Experimental mortality is most serious when
   *a. survivors might represent groups that are quite different from the unbiased groups that began the experiment.
   b. subjects are selected on the basis of extreme scores.
   c. extraneous variables are controlled.
   d. there is no treatment verification.

16. What threat to validity most likely influences a pre-test/posttest equivalent groups design?
   a. Selection bias
   b. Statistical regression.
   *c. Interaction of testing and treatment.
   d. History.

17. Which is not a characteristic of the Solomon four-groups design?
   a. All four groups receive posttest.
   b. It is possible to evaluate the effects of testing, history and maturation.
   *c. The two experimental groups receive pre-tests.
   d. A major difficulty is finding enough subjects to randomly assign them to four equivalent groups.

18. Which threat to internal validity cannot be controlled for by the use of random assignment?
   a. Selection bias.
   b. Statistical regression.
   *c. Unstable instrumentation.
   d. maturation.

19. A blind helps to prevent
   a. interaction of selection and maturation.
   b. interaction effect of testing.
   *c. experimenter bias.
   d. none of the above.

20. Pre-experimental designs
   *a. lack control groups or fail to provide for the equivalence of a control group.
   b. employ random assignment and the use of a control group.
   c. provide for a comparison of control groups before experimentation.
   d. none of the above.

21. Which is not a characteristic of the posttest only, equivalent groups design?
   a. Experimental and control groups are equated by random assignment.
   b. experimental and control groups both receive a posttest.
   c. The control group does not get the treatment.
   *d. Analysis of covariance is employed to equate the experimental and control groups.

22. Which is not a characteristic of quasi-experimental designs?
    *a. Equivalence of experimental and control groups is assured by random assignment.
    b. It involves naturally assembled groups such as intact classes which may be similar.
    c. It sometimes uses the same group as both the experimental and control group.
    d. Results of quasi-experimentation must be interpreted very cautiously.

23. The time series design
    *a. requires periodic observations of an individual or group.
    b. requires baseline data.
    c. minimizes the effect of history.
    d. can show rates of change.

24. Which is not a characteristic of the equivalent materials, pre-test/posttest design?
    *a. It controls for the threats of history and maturation.
    b. It is often difficult to select equated materials to be learned.
    c. A series of replications, through the process of rotation, can improve its validity.
    d. all of the above.

25. Which is not a characteristic of counterbalanced designs?
    a. Each subject receives all the treatment conditions.
    b. All groups receive all the treatments but in different orders.
    *c. Random assignment is employed.
    d. It is assumed that the different treatments will not interfere too much with each other.

26. Factorial designs
    a. are necessary when more than one independent variable is included in study.
    b. permit the researcher to determine significant main effects and interaction effects.
    c. permit more than two conditions of each variable.
    d. a and b.
    *e. all of the above.

Use the following to answer questions 27-32:

A debate coach in a large high school thinks that watching videotapes of high school debates will improve the performance of the team. She decides that half the team will watch videotapes of five debates prior to the first debate of the season while the other half does not watch any debates. She will then compare the performance of group A, those who watched the debates, and group B, those who did not watch the debates.

27. This study would be classified as:
   a. a school survey.
   b. an ex post facto study.
   c. a correlational study.
   d. a trend study.
   *e. experimental research.

28. In order to test her hypothesis, the coach should have which group watch the debates?
   a. The best debaters.
   b. The poorest debaters.
   *c. A randomly selected group.
   d. Those who volunteer.

29. The control group would be those who
   a. watch the debates.
   *b. do not watch the debates.
   c. try out for the debate team.
   d. are willing to cooperate in the study.
   e. do well in their debates.

30. The design of the study would be classified as
   a. one group pretest-posttest equivalent groups design.
   b. pretest-posttest equivalent groups design.
   *c. posttest only equivalent groups design.
   d. Solomon four-croup design.

31. The external validity question in this study would be:
   a. Was watching debates really responsible for differences in debate performance?
   b. was the coach unethical in making debaters watch debates?
   c. is watching the videotape debates worth the expense?
   *d. would watching debates improve the performance of other debate teams?

32. The independent variable is
   *a. watching debates.
   b. debate performance.
   c. the size of the school.
   d. the class ranking of the debaters.

Use the following to answer questions 33-34:

On the basis of their extremely low scores on a test of arithmetic, 20 third grade students were selected for a special six-week remedial arithmetic treatment. At the conclusion of the treatment, the 20 students were retested with the same instrument and the scores of the pretest and posttest were compared. The average improvement between the pretest and the posttest was ten points which was found to be statistically significant.

33. The teacher concludes that the observed improvement was due to the remedial treatment. However, which of the following is the greatest threat to the internal validity of the results?
 *a. Regression to the mean.
 b. Lack of random selection from an appropriate population of third graders.
 c. Interaction effect of testing.
 d. Interference of prior treatment.
 e. Experimental mortality.

34. Which of the following is the most effective way of eliminating the primary threat to internal validity?
 a. Random selection from all third graders.
 b. The addition of a control group selected randomly from all third graders.
 c. Eliminating the pretest.
 *d. The addition of a control group composed of students equal in tested arithmetic achievement to those receiving the treatment.
 e. None of the above.

35. Which of the following is the most effective way of eliminating testing as a threat to internal validity in an experimental design?
 a. Elimination of a pretest.
 b. Random selection of subjects from an appropriate population.
 c. Addition of a control group.
 *d. A and c are both effective.
 e. All of the above.

Essay Test Items and Topics for Class Discussion:

1. Why is the use of a control group so important in a true experiment? Discuss the advantages of the true experiment and the threats to validity it may control.

2. Discuss two examples of potential or past educational research studies and describe how the Hawthorne effect could confound their results.

3. What could you use as a placebo for the control group in the studies you have selected in the preceding question? What intervening and extraneous variables must you be aware of? How can you best control extraneous variables that endanger the internal validity of your study? What research design best fits your selected study?

4. Which threats to internal validity are controlled for by random assignment? By the use of a control group?

5. Discuss the difficulties of eliminating the threats of experimental artificiality and treatment verification in any study. What are some possible ways to overcome them?

6. Analyze two published research studies to determine whether the authors supplied the readers with accurate and unambiguous operational definitions of the variables in the study.

7. Give examples of common teacher-made one shot case studies and tell how they can be improved.

8. Design a time-series study that will address a common classroom problem. What are the possible threats that might confound your results?

9. Construct a factorial design that will address a common classroom problem. How many cells will you need to employ? Why?

10. In what areas of a school curricula can a researcher conveniently implement an equivalent materials, single group, pre-test/posttest design? How would you implement replications? How would you control threats to internal validity?

CHAPTER 7

SINGLE-SUBJECT EXPERIMENTAL RESEARCH

Key Definitions and Concepts

N of one research
behavior modification
experimental analysis of behavior
applied behavior analysis
repeated measurement
baselines
manipulating variables
intervention
phase length
carryover effect
alternating treatments
counterbalancing
transfer of training
response maintenance
assessment

observation
target behavior
operant rate
frequency measure
duration
real-time observation
response-specific measures
reliability
validity
A-B-A designs
multiple-baseline designs
withdrawal
replication designs
evaluating data

Multiple-Choice Test Items

1. Many critics of single-subject research question its
   *a. generalization to other subjects
   b. internal validity
   c. theoretical basis
   d. withdrawal phase in A-B-A designs

2. Single-subject research designs are similar to the following quasi-experimental design:
   a. time series design
   b. equivalent samples design
   c. equivalent materials, pretest, posttest design
   *d. all of the above.

3. The most common measurement tool used in single-subject research is
   a. a test
   b. a survey
   *c. observation
   d. a sociometric scale
   e. all of the above are equally common

4. Ideally the repeated measurements should take place:
   a. at the same time of day
   b. in the same setting
   c. by several different observers
   *d. a and b
   e. b and c

5. The baseline in single-subject research
   a. is analogous to the pretest in group designs
   b. may be repeated
   c. should be continued until the data are stable
   *d. all of the above

6. A baseline must include a minimum of ____ separate observations
   a. two
   *b. three
   c. four
   d. five

7. Assessment of the effect of an intervention in single subject research is usually accomplished by
   a. administering a posttest
   *b. observing the behavior under study
   c. interviewing the subject of the study
   d. interviewing the subject's parents and/or teacher

8. The target behavior
   a. may be an inappropriate behavior to be eliminated
   b. may be a behavior that the researcher wishes the subject to perform more frequently
   c. needs to be operationally defined
   d. a and b
   *e. all of the above

9. In single-subject research, the operational definition
   *a. should only refer to observable aspects of behavior
   b. may include references to intent
   c. should leave the observer with some flexibility
   d. all of the above
   e. none of the above

10. A frequency measure is
   *a. a simple count of the number of occurrences of the behavior that are observed during a given period of time
   b. the actual amount of time during which the individual performed the behavior
   c. a method in which the observation period is divided into brief observation/nonobservation intervals and the observer counts the number of observation intervals during which the behavior occurred
   d. a procedure in which behaviors are recorded in their actual frequency, duration, and order
   e. none of the above

11. Duration is an observation method that uses
   a. a simple count of the number of occurrences of the behavior that are observed during a given period of time
   *b. the actual amount of time during which the individual performed the behavior
   c. a method in which the observation period is divided into brief observation/nonobservation intervals and the observer counts the number of observation intervals during which the behavior occurred
   d. a procedure in which behaviors are recorded in their actual frequency, duration, and order
   e. none of the above

12. Time sampling is an observation method that uses
   a. a simple count of the number of occurrences of the behavior that are observed during a given period of time
   b. the actual amount of time during which the individual performed the behavior
   *c. a method in which the observation period is divided into brief observation/nonobservation intervals and the observer counts the number of observation intervals during which the behavior occurred
   d. a procedure in which behaviors are recorded in their actual frequency, duration, and order
   e. none of the above

13. Real-time observation uses
   a. a simple count of the number of occurrences of the behavior that are observed during a given period of time
   b. the actual amount of time during which the individual performed the behavior
   c. a method in which the observation period is divided into brief observation/nonobservation intervals and the observer counts the number of observation intervals during which the behavior occurred
   *d. a procedure in which behaviors are recorded in their actual frequency, duration, and order
   e. none of the above

14. A response specific measure is
    a. a simple count of the number of occurrences of the behavior that are observed during a given period of time
    b. the actual amount of time during which the individual performed the behavior
    c. a method in which the observation period is divided into brief observation/nonobservation intervals and the observer counts the number of observation intervals during which the behavior occurred
    d. a procedure in which behaviors are recorded in their actual frequency, duration, and order
    *e. none of the above

15. In an A-B-A-B design the Bs stand for
    *a. intervention
    b. baseline
    c. withdrawal
    d. b and c

16. In an A-B-A-B design the As stand for
    a. intervention
    b. baseline
    c. withdrawal
    *d. b and c

17. Multiple baseline designs use multiple
    a. subjects
    b. settings
    c. behaviors
    *d. any of the above

18. The data from single-subject research is usually evaluated by
    a. careful statistical analyses
    b. comparison with other studies
    *c. visual inspection of graphs
    d. the data are not evaluated

Essay Test Items and Topics for Class Discussion

1. Discuss a research problem that could be addressed using a single-subject design and how it could also be addressed with a group design. Which design would be preferable?

2. Analyze two published single subject studies to determine whether the authors used accurate and unambiguous operational definitions of the behaviors under study.

3. Design a single-subject study that addresses a common classroom problem. What are the possible threats that might confound your results?

4. Design a single-subject study in which two interventions are compared. What is the most serious threat that might confound your results? What could be done to lessen this threat?

5. For a single research problem, describe a potential A-B-A-B design and a potential multiple baseline that address the problem. Which design is better able to address the problem?

CHAPTER 8

QUALITATIVE RESEARCH

Key Definitions and Concepts

logico-positivism
phenomenological inquiry
research strategies
   document or content analysis
   case study
   ethnographic study
data collection techniques
   in-depth interviews
   direct observation
   written documents
   projective techniques
   questionnaires and surveys

qualitative themes
   naturalistic inquiry
   qualitative data
   context sensitivity
   unique case orientation
   design flexibility
   holistic perspective
theoretical traditions
   systems theory
   phenomenology
   heuristics
   ecological psychology

Multiple-Choice Test Items

1. Documentary analysis
   a. is used to describe prevailing practices or conditions.
   b. must subject documents to the same types of criticism employed by the historian.
   c. is not used to explain the possible causal factors related to some outcome, action, or event.
   *d. a and b.
   e. all of the above.

2. An appropriate ethnographic study requires
   a. the researcher to become aligned with either authority figures or the subjects.
   b. an initial hypothesis about the subjects under study.
   c. the use of quantitative analysis.
   *d. the researcher to interpret events and behaviors in terms of both his or her own view of the situation and that of the subjects.

3. The growth of foreign students in the graduate study programs of a particular state would best be determined by
   a. an ex post facto study.
   b. an ethnographic study.
   *c. a trend study.
   d. none of the above.

43

4. To assess the influence of newspaper editorials on current municipal election results, a researcher might include
   a. an activity analysis.
   b. a trend study.
   *c. a document analysis.
   d. an ethnographic study.

5. The assumption that human behavior is influenced by the setting in which it occurs is most important to
   a. a follow-up study.
   b. content analysis.
   *c. an ethnographic study.
   d. quota sampling.

6. Unlike persons conducting other forms of research, ethnographic researchers
   a. do not take a position of neutrality.
   b. defer their interpretations to the conclusions of the study.
   *c. begin with no hypotheses.
   d. all of the above.

7. Which is not a characteristic of a case study?
   a. It probes deeply and examines the social unit as a whole.
   b. The social unit may be a person, family, social group, institution, or a community.
   c. It analyzes interactions between the factors that explain present status.
   *d. It is less susceptible to a post hoc fallacy than other types of research.

8. A study a best schools practices using a systems theory approach would be most interested in
   a. the data regarding student test scores.
   b. teacher performance.
   c. the administrative structure of the school.
   d. the environment of the school.
   *e. all of the above which are important components of a systems theory approach.

9. Qualitative research methods is often described by what it isn't, quantitative. This is
   a. a problem in identifying what it really is.
   b. a moot point.
   c. currently being changed to be more descriptive
   *d. a and b

10. Case studies may make use of
    a. quantitative data.
    b. ethnographic data.
    c. document analysis.
    d. interviews.
    *e. all of the above.

11. Potential problems with case studies include:
 *a. the researcher must be skillful in separating the significant variables from those that are irrelevant.
 b. the researcher must be a skilled statistician.
 c. the researcher must randomly select the "case" to be studied.
 d. the researcher must predict outcomes prior to the study.

12. Good qualitative research will include a variety of data collection techniques.
 *a. true.
 b. false.

13. The use of multiple data collection techniques to verify each other is known as:
 a. collation of data
 *b. triangulation.
 c. organizing the data.
 d. detailed notation.

14. Ethnographic research methods derive primarily from anthropology.
 *a. true.
 b. false.

15. A term often used to describe qualitative data is "thick description.
 *a. true.
 b. false.

16. Qualitative research differs from quantitative research in that qualitative research requires the complete objectivity of the researcher.
 a. true.
 *b. false.

17. A case study is a good technique for generalization of the findings.
 a. true.
 *b. false.

18. Case studies are most useful in
 a. finding generalizable data.
 b. emphasizing in depth analysis.
 c. finding out a great deal about an individual or a community.
 *d. b and c.
 e. all of the above.

19. Ethnographic research is particularly important because
 a. human behavior is influenced by the setting.
 b. ethnographers can verify their previous hypotheses.
 c. hypotheses are generated and tested as the study proceeds.
 *d. a and c.

20. The various facets of qualitative data analysis do not include:
   a. organization of the data.
  *b. statistical analysis.
   c. description of the pertinent aspects of the study.
   d. interpretation.

Essay Test Items and Topics for Class Discussion

1. Why does the strength of an ethnographic study depend on the observation of natural behavior in a real-life setting?

2. Describe an educational problem or practice in which documentary analysis would yield useful information.

3. Design an ethnographic study of a particular segment of society with which you are very familiar and describe who would be your first contacts in order to gain access. Defend your selections.

4. What precautions should be considered when conducting a case study?

5. What are the major themes of qualitative research methods? Select two and describe how they are interrelated.

6. Why might a systems theory approach be the most effective way of examining the various components of school effectiveness? How might you combine various methods (e.g., case study, ethnography) to study school effectiveness?

CHAPTER 9

METHODS AND TOOLS OF RESEARCH

Key Definitions and Concepts:

nominal scale
ordinal scale
interval scale
ratio scale
qualitative studies
psychological studies
psychological inventories
performance vs. paper and pencil tests
standardized vs. non-standardized
   tests
achievement tests
aptitude tests
interest inventories
projective devices
   methods:
      association
      completion
      role-playing
      creative or constructive
types of test reliability:
   test-retest
   parallel or equivalent form
   internal consistency
   inter-scorer reliability
   standard error of measurement

Sources of validity evidence:
   content
   construct (internal structure)
   relations to other variables
      predictive and concurrent
test economy
observation in research
recording observations
sociometry
systematization of data collection
checklists
rating scales
score card
scaled specimens
characteristics of good observation
closed and open form questionnaires
characteristics of a good questionnaire
Thurstone technique
Likert method
semantic differential
validity and reliability issues of the
interview
Q methodology
self-concept Q-sort
sociogram

Multiple-Choice Test Items:

1. Why is there merit in using multiple methods?
   *a. Because each data-gathering device has its own particular bias.
   b. Because supplementing several methods eliminates bias.
   c. Because it generates more accurate data.
   d. None of the above.

2. Reliability
   a. is that quality of a data-gathering device or procedure that enables it to
      measure what it is supposed to measure.
   *b. is the quality of consistency that the instrument or procedure
      demonstrates.
   c. is a sufficient condition for validity.
   d. is none of the above

3. Which of the following scales provides the most precise information?
   a. Nominal.
   b. Ordinal.
   c. Interval.
   *d. ratio

4. Which is not a true statement concerning nominal scales and data?
   a. Nominal data are counted data.
   b. Nominal scales are non-orderable.
   c. Nominal scales are the least precise method of quantification.
   *d. Individuals may be assigned to more than one category represented in the nominal scale.

5. Which is not a true statement concerning ordinal scales and data?
   a. Ordinal scales permit ranking of items or individuals from highest to lowest.
   b. Ordinal scales have no absolute values.
   *c. Real differences between adjacent ranks are always equal.
   d. The criterion for highest to lowest ordering is expressed as relative positions or ranks in a group.

6. Which is not a true statement concerning interval scales and data?
   a. An interval scale lacks a true zero and cannot measure the complete absence of a trait.
   b. An interval scale is based on equal units of measurement indicating how much of the trait is present.
   *c. A score of 90 means that a person has twice as much of the trait as someone with a score of 45.
   d. An interval scale yields more relevant information than nominal and ordinal scales.

Match the following terms with the sentences that best describe them. (items 7-17)

a. closed form
b. open form
c. Likert method
d. semantic differential
e. Q methodology
f. sociometry
g. sociogram
h. guess-who technique
i. social distance scale
j. tabulation
k. crossbreaks

48

7. Process of transferring data from the data-gathering instruments to the tabular form in which they may be systematically examined. (j)

8. Closely related to sociometry, this technique consists of descriptions of the various roles played by children in a group. (h)

9. A tabular way of presenting observations and is a useful device in organizing and describing a data relationship. (k)

10. This technique provides an equal number of favorable and unfavorable statements which the individual rates on scale from strongly agree to strongly disagree. (c)

11. Method of ranking attitudes of judgments in which cards or slips of paper bearing the statements or items are arranged in a series of numbered piles. (e)

12. Questionnaires that call for a free response in the respondents' own words. (b)

13. Technique for describing social relationships that exist between individuals in a group.   (f)

14. Attempts to measure the degree to which an individual or group of individuals is accepted or rejected by another individual or group. (i)

15. Questionnaires that call for short check responses. (a)

16. A graphic representation of social relationship choices. (q)

17. Provides the individual with a seven-point scale with two adjectives, one at either end of the scale. (d)

18. In general, the smaller the percentage of responses to a questionnaire,
   a. the less significant the study.
   *b. the smaller the degree of confidence one may place in the adequacy of the data collected.
   c. the more we have predictive validity.
   d. all of the above.

19. Which is a true statement concerning ratio scales?
   a. Numerals of the ratio scale have the qualities of real numbers.
   b. Ratio scales are the most precise scales.
   c. Ratio scales are not capable of indicating the complete absence of a property.
   *d. a and b are both true.
   e. all of the above

20. Qualitative studies
   a. never use numerical measures.
   b. can only use nominal data.
   c. differ from quantitative studies in their techniques of observation.
   *d. are those in which description of observations are not ordinarily expressed in quantitative terms.

21. Psychological tests
   a. are designed to describe and measure a sample of behaviors limited to academic achievement.
   *b. yields objective and standardized descriptions of behavior.
   c. are not used to describe prevailing conditions at a particular time.
   d. all of the above.

22. Validating performance tests against paper and pencil tests or short tests against longer tests is an example of
   a. content evidence.
   *b. concurrent evidence.
   c. predictive evidence.
   d. construct evidence.

23. Which is not true of construct evidence?
   a. It is the degree to which scores on a test can be accounted for by the explanatory constructs of a sound theory.
   b. It is the degree to which an instrument's scores are systematically related to the judgments made by observation of behavior identified by a theory as dominant.
   *c. Intelligence tests require adequate construct validity but it is not particularly important for aptitude tests.
   d. It is particularly important for personality tests.

24. Which is not a characteristic of content evidence?
   *a. It is just as important for aptitude tests as for achievement tests.
   b. Its criterion is often assessed by a panel of experts who judge its adequacy and express it by numerical measurement.
   c. It shows how adequately the test samples the universe of knowledge and skills that a student is expected to master.
   d. None of the above.

25. Which is not a characteristic of personality inventories?
   a. These instruments yield scores which are assumed or have been shown to measure certain personality traits or tendencies.
   b. Because of the difficulty, inability or unwillingness of individuals to report their own reactions accurately or objectively, these instruments are of limited value.
   c. Some of these instruments have reasonable empirical validity with particular groups of individuals but prove to be invalid when applied to others.
   *d. The development of instruments of personality description and measurement has a long and rich history that makes it possible to base the instrument's assumptions on adequate theories of personality.

26. Which is not a characteristic of projective devices?
   a. They attempt to disguise their purpose so completely in order to counteract the subject's tendency to try to appear in the best light concerning how they believe they are expected to respond.
   b. These devices enable subjects to unconsciously reveal internal feelings, attitudes, values, or wishes to an external referent.
   *c. A projective device is free of the limitations characteristic of personality inventories concerning the validity of contemporary personality theories.
   d. Association techniques, completion techniques, and role-playing are often part of projective devices.

27. Which is not a characteristic of aptitude tests?
   a. They differ from achievement in that they measure nondeliberate or unplanned learning.
   b. They may be used to divide students into relatively homogeneous groups for instructional purposes.
   c. They are highly controversial when used for the purposes of placement and classification.
   *d. Aptitude instruments are not used to predict ability in the area of musical and artistic pursuits.

28. Which is not a characteristic of interest inventories?
   a. Some of these instruments compare the subject's patterns of interest to the interest patterns of successful practitioners in a number of vocational fields.
   b. It is assumed that the subject will find his or her area of greatest interest where percentile scores are relatively high.
   *c. These self-report instruments are used as unstandardized interviews.
   d. Some of these instruments are based on the correlation between a number of activities from the areas of school, recreation. and work.

Match the following terms with the correct passages that describe them. (items 29-34)

a. aptitude tests
b. achievement test
c. projective devices
d. interest inventories

29. This instrument attempts to measure the level of an individual performance. (b)

30. This instrument attempts to predict the degree of achievement that may be expected from an individual in a particular activity. (a)

31. This instrument attempts to yield a measure of the types of activities that an individual has a tendency to like and choose. (d)

32. This instrument attempts to yield data that the subject may only unconsciously reveal about themselves. (c)

33. This instrument attempts to predict an individual's capacity to acquire improved performance with additional training. (a)

34. Role playing and constructive techniques are often used in this instrument. (c)

35. Which is a characteristic of achievement tests?
    a. They are often used in evaluating the influences of courses of study, teachers, and teaching methods.
    b. Most tests used in school are achievement tests.
    c. In using these instruments, it is important to generalize the effects of achievement beyond the specific elements being measured.
    *d. a and b.
    e. All of the above.

36. Construct evidence is particularly important for
    a. achievement tests.
    b. personality tests.
    c. aptitude tests.
    *d. both b and c.
    e. all of the above.

Match the following terms with the correct passages that describe them. (items 37-42)

a. test-retest reliability
b. equivalent or parallel form reliability
c. split-halves reliability
d. Kuder Richardson formula
e. inter-scorer reliability
f. standard error of measurement

37. Scores on the first half of the test are correlated with scores on the second half of that test. (c)

38. Two or more persons independently score the same set of tests or observations. (e)

39. Two or more forms that are supposed to be used interchangeably are compared. (b)

40. A mathematical test that results in the average correlation of all possible split half correlations. (d)

41. Scores on a test are highly correlated with scores on a second administration of that test to the same subjects at a later date. (a)

42. A statistic that permits the interpretation of an individual's score obtained on a test. (f)

Essay Test Items and Topics for Class Discussion:

1. Why is it sometimes advisable to omit from analyses those scores near the middle of the distribution?

2. What is the utility of percentage comparisons?

3. What are the limitations of percentage comparisons?

4. How are validity and reliability achieved in questionnaires?

5. How is it possible to estimate the predictive validity of some types of questionnaires?

6. Discuss the characteristics of a good questionnaire. What suggestions are helpful in preparing and administering the questionnaire?

7. Discuss some of the characteristics of skillful interviewing.

8. Why is recording interviews on tape preferred to note-taking?

9. What important distinction is made between performance tests and paper and pencil tests?

10. Why are personality inventories of limited value?

11. Which is more difficult to determine in observational and questionnaire techniques -- validity or reliability? Defend your selection.

12. Why is it necessary to carefully define operationally the variables of a study which cannot be observed directly?

13. Why are some behavioral scientists concerned that excessive emphasis on quantification may result in the measurement of fragmentary qualities not relevant to real behavior?

14. What important distinction is made between power tests and timed or speed tests?

15. What important distinctions are made between standardized and non-standardized tests?

16. Discuss what is meant by: "reliability is necessary but not sufficient condition of validity."

17. Why is observation as research technique so difficult to carry out well?

18. How can reliability among observers be demonstrated?

19. Discuss the limitations of rating scales.

20. What are the advantages of personally administering questionnaires to groups of individuals?

21. Discuss the limitations of the Likert method.

22. Discuss the principles the text suggests that can be employed to make questionnaire items more precise. (Note: the book discusses eleven such principles).

CHAPTER 10

DESCRIPTIVE DATA ANALYSIS

Key Definitions and Concepts:

statistic
parameter
parametric data
non-parametric data
descriptive analysis
inferential analysis
the array
grouped data distributions
frequency tables
mean
median
mode
bimodal distribution
multimodal distribution
range
deviation from the mean
variance
standard deviation
the normal distribution
non-normal distributions
skewed distributions
practical applications of the normal
   curve
standard scores
the sigma score (Z)

T score (T)
the College Board score (Zcb)
percentile rank
correlation
the scattergram
the linear regression line
plotting the slope of the
   regression line
Pearson's Product Moment
   Coefficient (r)
Spearman rank order coefficient of
   correlation
interpretation of a correlation
   coefficient
misinterpretations of a correlation
   coefficient
prediction of unknown Y values from
   known X values
standard error of estimate
the coefficient of validity
the coefficient of reliability
test-retest correlation
equivalent forms correlation
split-halves correlation
limitations of statistics

Multiple-Choice Test Items:

1. As a coefficient of correlation increases,
   *a. its ability to predict increases.
    b. prediction error is eliminated.
    c. prediction error increases.
    d. Sest = Sy

2. Parametric data is distinguished from non-parametric data because
parametric statistical tests
    a. are only concerned with sample populations.
   *b. assume the data are normally or near-normally distributed.
    c. are distribution-free tests.
    d. require either counted or ranked data.

55

3. Inferential analysis
   a. limits generalization to the particular group of individuals observed.
   b. produces data that describe one group and that group only.
  *c. involves the process of sampling in order to draw conclusions about a population.
   d. all of the above.

4. Which of the following statements is correct concerning a coefficient of orrelation?
   a. It suggests a cause-and-effect relationship between variables.
   b. Negative correlation suggests no causation is possible.
   c. Zero correlation suggests no causation is possible.
  *d. An important use of the coefficient of correlation is for the prediction of unknown Y values from known X values.

5. A parameter
   a. is a measure based on observation of the characteristics of a sample.
   b. is used to estimate statistics computed from a sample.
  *c. is characteristic of a population generally inferred from sample data.
   d. is used to estimate statistics computed from a population.

6. The mode of a set of scores is 82. This means
   a. half of the scores were above 82. and half were below.
   b. the median should be used because the distribution is skewed.
   c. there will be greater error variance.
  *d. the score of 82 occurs most frequently in this distribution.

7. A test that is extremely easy tends to be
   a. positively skewed.
  *b. negatively skewed.
   c. normally distributed.
   d. none of the above.

8. If a researcher discovers a sample that consists of persons from two distinct populations, he or she might expect
   a. a normal distribution.
   b. a multimodal distribution.
  *c. a bimodal distribution.
   d. less variance between populations.

9. Variance
   a. is equal to the sum of the deviations.
  *b. describes how all the scores are dispersed about the mean.
   c. is dependent on the magnitude of the mean.
   d. expresses any score in a distribution in terms of its distance from the median.

10. Which is not a characteristic of a normal distribution?
   a. The mean, mode and median have the same value.
   b. The scores cluster around the mean.
   c. It is symmetrical around the vertical axis.
  *d. The distribution curve is bounded in either direction.

11. Students who have low intelligence quotients tend to score low on mathematics tests. This relationship is an example of
  *a. a positive correlation.
   b. a negative correlation.
   c. a perfect correlation.
   d. a chance correlation

12. A teacher concludes that the more hours she had her students practice the piano, the fewer errors they made when learning new pieces. This relationship is an example of
   a. a positive correlation.
  *b. a negative correlation.
   c. a perfect correlation.
   d. a chance correlation

13. Spearman's rank order coefficient of correlation
   a. is useful for teachers when conducting studies using a single classroom group of students as subjects.
   b. is an acceptable method if data are available only in ordinal form.
   c. will yield the same score as Pearson's r if there are no tie scores.
  *d. all of the above.

14. In a study of the relationship between smoking and frequency of heart attacks, a researcher reports a strong positive relationship. Which of the following correlation coefficients would be most likely to represent the relationship?
   a. -.80
   b. .07
   c. 1.15
   d. -.01
  *e. .68

Use the following to answer questions 15 and 16.

A large survey of college freshman at eight institutions report that the correlation between combined SAT scores and freshman year grade point average is .30.

15. What proportion of the total variance in grade point average is accounted for or explained by combined SAT scores?
   a. .30
   *b. .09
   c. .70
   d. .07

16. What proportion of the total variance in freshman grade point average is explained by variables or factors other than combined SAT scores?
   *a. .91
   b. .70
   c. .30
   d. .40

Use the following to answer questions 17 and 18.

In studying the correlates of tested intelligence on a sample of 10,000 college freshmen randomly selected from all entering freshmen in the country, sociologists report a correlation of .26 between socioeconomic status (SES) and scores on the Stanford Binet Intelligence Test. The correlation is statistically significant at the .05 level.

17. Which of the following is the most accurate explanation of what the statistically significant correlation means in the above study?
   a. The correlation is very important.
   *b. If the correlation between SES and intelligence in the population is .00, a sample correlation of .26 should be observed by chance in less than 5 in every 100 samples (of size 10,000).
   c. If the correlation between SES and intelligence in the population is .00, a sample correlation of .26 should be observed by chance in more than 5 in every 100 samples (of size 10,000).
   d. If the correlation between SES and intelligence in the population is .00, a sample correlation of .26 should be observed by chance in more than 95 in every 100 samples (of size 10,000).

18. Which of the following is the most appropriate conclusion drawn from the finding?
   a. Socioeconomic status causes variations in intelligence.
   b. The observed correlation is probably the result of sampling error and should be ignored.
   c. Intelligence causes variations in socioeconomic status.
   *d. Variations in socioeconomic status and intelligence tend to be positively related.
   e. Socioeconomic status and intelligence have no causal relationship.

19. A set of scores has a mean of 50 and a variance of 4. The standard deviation for this distribution is:
   *a. 2
   b. 54
   c. 16
   d. 10

20. Which of the following is most likely to have a distribution similar to the normal curve?
   a. Incomes of Atlanta adult males.
   *b. Heights of Atlanta adult males.
   c. Enrollments in grades 1-12 in the Atlanta school system.
   d. Population of incorporated cities in Georgia.
   e. Ages of Georgia school teachers.

21. About _____ percent of the scores fall between Z scores of plus and minus 1.0 on the   normal curve.
   a. 16
   b. 33
   c. 50
   *d. 68
   e. 98

22. On a test with a standard deviation of 20 and a mean of 80, an individual with a raw score of 70 will have a Z score of
   *a. -.5
   b. .5
   c. -1.0
   d. 1.0
   e. -1.5

23. The Pearson Product-Moment correlation cannot be used with
   a. interval data.
   b. ratio data.
   c. ordinal data.
   d. dichotomous data.
   *e. it can be used with all of the above.

Use the following data to answer Questions 24-26.

X
42
41
40
39
38
37
36

24. The mean of this distribution is
  a. 38.00
  b. 38.50
  *c. 39.00
  d. none of these

25. The mode of this distribution is
  a. 38.00
  b. 38.50
  c. 39.00
  *d. none of these

26. The median of this distribution is
  a. 38.00
  b. 38.50
  *c. 39.00
  d. none of these

27. If there is one very high score and a larger number of low scores distribution
  *a. the mean will be higher than the median.
  b. the median will be higher than the mean.
  c. the median and the mean will be the same.
  d. none of the above.

28. One would use a correlation coefficient to
  a. describe the typical performance of an individual student.
  b. describe the typical performance of a group of students.
  c. describe the position of a single student in a group of students.
  *d. describe the relationship between verbal aptitude scores and nursing skills.
  e. determine whether a distribution is normal or not.

29. A negative correlation is
  *a. as good for prediction as a positive correlation.
  b. indicative of no relationship between the variables under investigation.
  c. obtained when the distribution of measures on the two variables are not linear.
  d. none of the above.

30. If you have a Z score of +3.0 on this exam, your score is
  *a. very high.
  b. above average but not exceptionally high.
  c. about average.
  d. below average but not exceptionally low.
  e. very low.

Questions 31 and 32 are based on the following situation:

Five boys took a history test and a geography test with the following results:

| | History | | | Geography | |
	raw score	Z score		raw score	Z score
George	28	.5		85	1.5
Ralph	32	1.5		65	.5
David	26	0		55	0
Paul	20	-1.5		45	-.5
John	24	-.5		25	-1.5

$$\text{History}$$
$$\Sigma x = 130$$
$$\sigma = 4$$

$$\text{Geography}$$
$$\Sigma x = 275$$
$$\sigma = 20$$

31. The boy whose performance in history is most in agreement with his performance in geography is
   a. George
   b. Ralph
 *c. David
   d. Paul
   e. John

32. Since the history test mean is lower than the geography test mean, we would conclude
   a. these boys are better in history than in geography.
   b. these boys are better in geography than in history.
   c. their teacher has probably spent twice as much time on geography as he did on history.
   d. their teacher knows more geography than history.
 *e. none of the above.

33. Which one of these r's has the least predictive value?
   a. .91
   b. .50
 *c. .17
   d. -.23
   e. -1.00

34. A standard score with a mean of zero and a standard deviation of one is a
   a. T score.
 *b. Z score.
   c. t score.
   d. CEEB score.
   e. stanine score.

Computational Test Items

1. What is the mean, mode, median and range for the following set of scores?

X	Answers:
94	mean = 71.6
82	mode = 72
72	median = 70
72	range = 37
68	
65	
62	
58	

2. Compute the variance (σ^2) and the standard deviation (σ) for the following set of scores.

X	Answers:
98	$\sigma^2 = 97.64$
96	$\sigma = 9.88$
95	
90	
90	
87	
85	
81	
75	
70	
68	

3. Compute the standard deviation (S) for this sample.

X

90
85
75
70
70
65
60
55
50
50

Answer: S = 13.78

62

4. Given the following data, calculate the Z and T for the two children's scores on arithmetic and reading tests:

Arithmetic		Reading	
Child 1 score	= 72	Child 1 score	= 89
Child 2 Score	= 65	Child 2 score	= 104
Mean	= 69	Mean	= 93
Standard Deviation	= 4	Standard Deviation	= 6
Number Taking Test	= 16	Number Taking Test	= 14

Answers:

Z1 = 0.75	Z1 = -.67
T1 = 58.0	T1 = 43.0
Z2 = -1.0	Z2 = 1.83
T2 = 40.0	T2 = 68.0

5. If John ranks twenty-fourth in his senior class of 203 students, what is his percentile rank?

Answer: John's percentile rank is 88.

6. Calculate b, when r = .70 and X and Y have a standard deviation of 4 and 3 respectively.

Answer: b = .525

7. Find the Pearson product-moment correlation (r) for the following Z scores .

Z_x	Z_y
2.00	1.80
1.90	1.70
1.00	1.00
-.40	.95
-.50	-.10
-1.00	-.60
-1.30	-1.00

Answer: r = .94

8. Find the Pearson product-moment correlation (r) for the following set of raw scores using the deviation method.

X	Y
95	78
90	77
80	80
70	75
65	68
60	72
55	70

Answer: $r = .46$

9. Use the raw score method to find the correlation (r) for the following set of scores:

X	Y
85	76
84	78
75	77
76	71
70	75
69	73
68	72

Answer: $r = .005$

10. Discuss what is meant by each of the correlations you have just computed in questions 4, 5, and 6. Compute the coefficient of determination for each and determine what percent of the variance was not explained by the predictor variable. (If this test question is used after Chapter 11 has been covered, statistical significance may   also be requested).

Answer for question Number 4:

$r = .94$ = very high correlation
$r^2 = .88$ = coefficient of determination
$1 - r^2 = .12 = 12\%$ of the variance was *not* explained.

Answer for question Number 5:

$r = .46$ = moderate correlation
$r^2 = .21$ = coefficient of determination
$1 - r^2 = .79 = 79\%$ of the variance was not explained.

Answer for question Number 6:

$r = .005$ = negligible correlation
$r^2 = .00$ = coefficient of determination
$1 - r^2 = 1.00 = 100\%$ of the variance is still not explained.

11. Compute the Spearman rank order coefficient of correlation for the following data:

Subject	English	French
A	1	4
B	2	2
C	3	1
D	4	5
E	5	3
F	6	7
G	7	6

Answer: Rho = .64

12. Use a regression equation to predict a high school student's college freshman grade point average (GPA) given the following data.

$r = .62$ $X = 2.50$ (student's high school GPA)
$S_y = .50$ $X = 2.40$ (mean high school GPA).
$S_x = 40$ $Y = 2.80$ (mean college freshman GPA).

Answer: $Y = 2.88$
          $(b = .78)$
          $(a = .93)$

13. Estimate the prediction error of a score (Y) from a known score (X) when the correlation is .45 and the $S_y = 4$.

Answer: $S_{est_y} = 3.58$

14. You have used a split-half correlation to estimate the internal reliability of a test. How would you correct a correlation of +.75 and what would the new correlation be?

Answer: Use the Spearman-Brown prophecy formula. The adjusted correlation is $r = + .86$.

CHAPTER 11

INFERENTIAL DATA ANALYSIS

Key Definitions and Concepts:

inferential data analysis	student's distribution
statistical inference	t-critical values
the central limit theorem	homogeneity of variance
standard error of the mean	the F-ratio
parametric test assumptions	analysis of covariance
statistical significance	partial correlation
the t-test	analysis of variance
the null hypothesis	one-way analysis of variance
alpha levels of significance	between-group variance
Type I error	within-group variance
Type 11 error	factorial analysis of variance
one-tailed test of significance non	-parametric tests
two-tailed test of significance the	Chi Square test
degrees of freedom	Yate's Correction of Continuity
standard deviation for Samples (S)	the Mann-Whitney U test

Multiple-Choice Test Items:

1. A teacher who gives credit to a new program for academic gains has
    actually obtained those results by sampling error.
   *a. He has made a Type I error.
    b. He has made a Type 11 error.
    c. He can still claim that the gains are due to the program because other
        variables were controlled.
    d. none of the above.

2. Which of the following is not an assumption for parametric tests?
    a. The observations are independent.
    b. The samples have equal or near equal variance.
    c. The variables described are expressed in interval or ratio scales.
   *d. Data of this type are either counted or ranked.

3. Which statement concerning the null hypothesis is not true?
    a. It concerns a judgment as to whether apparent differences result from
        sampling error.
   *b. It is restricted to experimental studies.
    c. It is needed for statistical purposes.
    d. The standard of rejection or acceptance in psychological and educational
        circles is generally at the .05 alpha level of significance.

4. When researchers hypothesize a direction of difference,
   a. they expect the t critical values to be higher.
   *b. they should use a one-tailed test of significance.
   c. they should use a two-tailed test of significance.
   d. none of the above

5. As sample size increases
   *a. the probability of a correct prediction of an inferred value increases.
   b. the probability of a correct prediction of an inferred value decreases.
   c. the probability of a correct prediction of an inferred value remains the
      same.
   d. the chance of Type I errors increases.

6. What one condition must be met to justify the method of pooled variances
      applied in
      t-tests for small samples?
   a. Sampling error must be totally eliminated.
   *b. Homogeneity of the variances of the samples must be obtained.
   c. Researchers must use the .01 alpha level of significance.
   d. None of the above.

7. As sample size increases
   a. the standard error of the mean increases.
   *b. the standard error of the mean decreases.
   c. the standard error of the mean is unaffected.
   d. the standard error of the mean approaches the standard deviation of the
      sample.

8. Computing a number of separate t-tests to show the relationships of multiple
      independent variables with a dependent variable
   a. is preferable to using analysis of variance.
   *b. will increase the overall Type I error rate.
   c. will decrease the overall Type I error rate.
   d. none of the above.

9. In factorial analysis of variance,
   a. we employ multiple t-tests.
   b. we can analyze the effects of one independent variable on a single
      dependent variable.
   c. the total variance is divided into two parts.
   *d. the main effects and the interaction effects of two or more independent
      variables on a single dependent variable are analyzed.

10. Partial correlation is particularly useful when
   a. sample sizes are very small.
   b. sample sizes are very large.
   *c. the subjects in two or more groups are found to differ on a pre-test.
   d. the subjects in two or more groups are equivalent on a pre-test.

11. Residuals are
a. the scores corrected by t-tests.
*b. the scores corrected by analysis of covariance procedures.
c. the scores determined before inequalities are removed.
d. none of the above.

12. Analysis of covariance
a. is more robust than analysis of variance.
b. can transform a quasi-experiment into a true experiment.
c. is a substitute for randomization.
*d. is not as robust as analysis of variance.

13. If $r^2 = .49$, then
a. 49% of the variance of the dependent variable is due to factors other than Predictor variables.
b. 49% of the variance of the dependent variable is due to a single predictor variable.
*c. 49% of the variance of the dependent variable is due to the combination of two or more predictor variables.
d. 51% of the variance of the dependent variable is due to a single predictor variable.

14. When $r = 0$,
a. the variables are negatively correlated.
b. Sesty = 0
*c. Sesty = Sy
d. the best blind prediction of any Y from any X is + 1.

15. Which is not a characteristic of the Chi Square (χ^2) test?
a. It applies to discrete data, counted rather than measured values.
b. It is a test of the independence of one variable being unrelated to another variable.
*c. It is a measure of the degree of relationship between two variables.
d. It evaluates the probability that the observed relationship results from chance.

16. Which is not a characteristic of the Yate's Correction for Continuity formula?
a. It is a formula of χ^2 modified for cells with frequency counts of fewer than 10.
b. It involves only a 2 x 2 factorial of design.
*c. It always involves 2 degrees of freedom.
d. It is a measure of independence concerning variable relationships.

17. The 95% confidence interval for a sample with a mean of 20 and a standard error of 3 is:
a. 12.32 and 27.60
b. 17.00 and 23.00
c. 14.00 and 26.00
*d. 14.12 and 25.88

e. none of the above.

Use the following to respond to questions 18 and 19.

A researcher wants to assess the effects of a particular treatment on the subjects. Adopting a post-test only control group design he randomly selects 100 subjects from a known population and then randomly assigns So each to a treatment and to a control group. He calls this Study 1. He then repeats exactly the same design, selection, assignment, treatment and measurement in second study of the same population (Study 2). The two studies yield the following results.

Study 1	Study 2
treatment mean = 48.2	treatment mean = 48.0
treatment S = 5.1	treatment S = 10.9
control mean = 43.6	control mean = 43.4
control S = 5.8	control S = 10.2

18. In which of the two studies is the difference between treatment and control group means more likely to be statistically significant?
*a. Study
 b. Study 2
 c. Neither. The likelihood of a significant difference is about the same for both studies.

19. For statistically significant differences to be equally likely in both studies, which of the following would have to be true?
 a. The treatment and control group means in Study I would have to be further apart.
 b. The treatment and control group means in Study 2 would have to be further apart.
 c. The standard deviations in Study 2 would have to be smaller.
*d. Either b or c.
 e. Either a or c.

20. When the results of a study are reported to be statistically significant, this means that
 a. the results are meaningful and useful in a practical situation.
*b. similar results would probably be obtained with a new sample from the same population and the same procedure.
 c. the results were what was predicted by the hypothesis.
 d. the size of the difference between the groups was large.
 e. the results were surprising and did not correspond to theory.

21. When an F- or t-test indicates that a difference between two means is significant at less than the .05 level, one concludes that the difference could have occurred by chance
   a. more often than 1 time in 20;
*b. less often than 1 time in 20;
   c. more than 1 time in 5;
   d. less than 5 times in 1000.

Use the letter before the following five statistics to indicate the best one to use for each in answering the research hypotheses indicated for Questions 22 to 25.

   a. F-ratio
   b. Pearson r
   c. standard deviation
   d. t-test
   e. median

22. Any rise in teachers' income has been accompanied by an equivalent rise in cost of living. (b)

23. The mean grade point average for undergraduates in the education department is significantly higher than the mean GPA for undergraduate art students. (d)

24. The typical employee at the Bloomington RCA plant missed five days of work because of illness in 1979. (e)

25. Both average and above average second grade students make greater improvements in reading achievement when taught by the sight method instead of the phonetic method. (a)

26. Given the mean of a sample in a test as 25 and the standard deviation as 5, the standard error of the mean would be:
   a. 1
   b. 2
   c. 3
   d. 5
   e. impossible to calculate with the given information.

Computational Test Items:

1. Determine the 95% and 99% confidence intervals for a randomly selected sample when:

$X = 90$
$S = 22$
$N = 25$

Explain your answer.

95% is between 81.38 and 98.62 and
99% is between 78.65 and 101.35

Ninety-five times out of one hundred the mean of this sample's population will
fall between 81.38 and 98.62.

Ninety-nine times out of one hundred the mean of this sample's population will
fall between 78.62 and 101.35.

2. Calculate a t-test on the following data and determine if the result is
statistically significant.

Experimental Group   Control Group

  $N_1 = 30$ $N_2 = 34$

  $X_1 = 84$ $X_2 = 82$

  S $= 49$ $S2 = 64$

        $t = 1.07$
        $df = 30 + 34 - 2 = 62$

No significant difference, we fail to reject the null hypothesis.

3. The mean score of ten students on a reading test was compared with the
mean score of twelve students from another school on the same test. Both
groups were randomly selected. Test the null hypothesis that there is no
statistically significant difference between the mean test scores at the .01 and
.05 alpha levels of significance.

  School A   School B

  $X = 15$ $X = 10$

  $S2 = 25$ $S2 = 16$

  $N = 10$ $N = 12$

        Answer: $t = 2.63$ $df = 20$

t is significant at the .05 level. Reject the null only at .05 level.

4. Test the null hypothesis that there is no difference between the mean achievement of two groups, each made up of twenty students who were matched on the basis of IQs.

Exp. Group   Control Group

N = 20   N = 20

S2 = 49   S2 = 36

X = 76   X = 66

r = +.70
df = 38

Answer: t = 8.70. A t critical value of 8.70 does exceed or equal the critical values with 38 degrees of freedom for a two-tailed test of significance:
2.021 at .05 level   2.704 at .01 level
Reject the null hypothesis at the .01 level of probability.

5. Use a t test to test the significance of a Pearson Product Moment Correlation of r = .6 for a sample of 26 subjects.

Answer: Since there are 24 degrees of freedom, the t critical value must exceed or equal 2.064 at .05 level, and 2.797 at .01 Level.

The t value of 3.68 does exceed these critical values. Thus, the correlation of .60 is significant at the .01 Level of probability.

6. Given the following data, calculate the mean squares and F.

Source of Variance	SS	df	MS	F
Between Groups	312.6	2		
Within Groups	146.2	24		
Total	458.8			

Answers: MSb = 156.3
MSw = 6.09
F = 25.67 Statistically significant at the .01 Level

7. Given the following correlation coefficients, calculate the partial correlation of class attendance (X1), and reading achievement (X2), with age removed (X3).

r12 = .70
r13 = .55
r23 = .55

Answer: r12.3 = .57

8. Given the following data, calculate the predicted score (Y).

$$b1 = .41$$
$$b2 = .003$$
$$X1 = 3.1$$
$$X2 = 936$$
$$a = -1.93$$

Answer = $Y = .41 (3.1) + .003(936) - 1.93 = 2.15$

9. Compute the $\chi2$ value for the data represented in this crossbreak table and determine if these variables tend to be systematically related.

Students Home   Days of Absence From School
Living Situation

Lives with:	<16	16-25	26-35	Over 35	Totals
Both Parents	14	8	7	3	32
Mother Only	12	9	9	2	32
Father Only	10	10	11	4	35
Neither Parent	6	9	14	5	34
Totals	42	36	41	14	133

Answer: $\chi2 = 20.87$ degrees of freedom

The relationship is significant at the .05 level (critical value needed = 16.92) but is not significant at the .01 level (critical value needed = 21.67) with 9 degrees of freedom. These variables are systematically related at the .05 probability level.

10. Using the data in Question 10, determine if there is a relationship between a child living with neither parent and number of days he or she was absent from school.

Answer: Step One: collapse 16 cells into 8.

	<16	16-25	26-35	over 35	Totals
Neither	6	9	14	5	34
Other	36	27	27	9	99
Totals	42	36	41	14	133

$\chi2 = 6.79$ $df = 3$

This relationship is not significant at the .05 level (critical value needed = 7.82) or the .01 level (critical value needed = 11.34). These variables do exhibit the quality of independence and do not tend to be systematically related.

11. A principal wanted to determine if there was a relationship between student participation in after school sports and club activities and improved grade point averages.

	improved GPA	unimproved GPA	Totals
Participation	54	26	80
Non-participation	24	40	64
Totals	78	66	144

Answer: $\chi2 = 14.19$ df= 1

The relationship is significant at both the .05 (critical value needed = 3.84) and .01 levels (critical value needed = 6.64). The variables are related.

12. A learning disabilities resource room teacher wanted to determine if participation in after school intramural activities led to improved grades for her students. The teacher used the following data to test the hypothesis.

	improved GPA	not improved GPA	Totals
Participants	8	12	52
Non-participants	3	11	14
Totals	11	23	34

Answer: The Yates Correction for Continuity formula should be used.
$\chi2 = .59$

There is no significant relationship at either the .05 (critical value needed = 3.84) or .01 (critical value needed = 6.64) levels.

13. Use the Mann-Whitney formula to test the null hypothesis for the data samples   below.

$\underline{X}$ $\underline{C}$

X	C
80	81
79	82
78	83
77	87
76	88
62	89
61	74
63	73
71	54
75	55
51	41
52	42
53	43
64	44
92	46
90	47
31	48
84	45
85	49
86	50

Answers: $U_1 = 285$
$U_2 = 115$
$Z = 2.30$

Since the Z is greater than 1.96, the null hypothesis is rejected at the .05 level.

CHAPTER 12

COMPUTER DATA ANALYSIS

Key Definitions and Concepts:

computers   input
storage   output
data organization   "garbage in-garbage out"
Statistical Package for the Social Sciences (SPSS)

Multiple-Choice Test Items:

1. _____ entails entering information or data into the computer.
   a. Output
   b. Storage
   c. Control
   *d. Input
   e. None of the above

2. _____ is the process by which information is kept for later use.
   a. Output
   *b. Storage
   c. Control
   d. Input
   e. None of the above

3. _____ is the process by which data are organized.
   a. Output
   b. Storage
   c. Control
   d. Input
   *e. None of the above.

4. The_____ or retrieval process transfers the processed information
         from the   computer to the researcher.
   *a. output
   b. storage
   c. control
   d. input
   e. None of the above.

5. When using a computer to carry out the data analyses, the researcher must
       write his or her own program.
   a. True
   *b. False

76

6. The first step in using a computer to calculate statistical analyses is
   a. put the data into the computer.
   b. select the appropriate software.
   *c. organize and code the data.
   d. write the control cards for the program.
   e. it doesn't matter in which order the above four steps are accomplished.

Topics for Take home Test or Homework:

The most efficacious way to determine if the students understand this material is to have them actually use the computer to calculate data analyses. Thus, the instructor of the course may wish to have the students carry out a number of computer analyses. We suggest that the students be given a data set with at least five variables and 30 subjects (or use the data provided in Appendix B of the text which contains 6 variables and 100 subjects). The students may then be assigned specific packaged programs, such as the examples in the text, to carry out on the data. The students should create their own variable names and write a one to two page report of the results of each analysis on "their" data set. This will provide them with experience in using the computer and in writing results of data analyses.

Of course, the students will need more than this text to be able to accomplish the above suggestions. A session should be conducted on the statistical program on the computer (usually a PC or Macintosh) to be used. While this assignment may not be realistic (in terms of time) for the course in which this text is required, it is a very useful assignment for students who will be conducting research and writing theses and dissertations.

Teaching Tips for First-time Instructors and Adjunct Professors

Teaching Tips Contents

1. How to be an Effective Teacher
Seven principles of good teaching practice
Tips for Thriving: Creating an Inclusive Classroom

2. Today's Undergraduate Students
Traditional students
Nontraditional students
Emerging influences
What students want from college professors
Tips for Thriving: Be a "Facilitator of Learning"

3. Planning Your Course
Constructing the syllabus
Problems to avoid
Tips for Thriving: Visual Quality

4. Your First Class
Seven goals for a successful first meeting
Tips for Thriving: An Icebreaker

5. Strategies for Teaching and Learning
Getting participation through active learning
Team learning
Tips for Thriving: Active Learning and Lecturing

6. Grading and Assessment Techniques
Philosophy of grading
Criterion grading
Tips for Thriving: Result Feedback

7. Using Technology
Advice on using the web in small steps
Tips for Thriving: Using Videos

8. Managing Problem Situations
Cheating
Unmotivated students
Credibility problems
Tips for Thriving: Discipline

9. Surviving When You're Not Prepared
Contingency plans

10. Improving Your Performance
Self evaluation
Tips for Thriving: Video-Recording Your Class

Teaching Tips for First-time Instructors and Adjunct Professors

1   How to be an Effective Teacher

(Adapted from Royse, *Teaching Tips for College and University Instructors: A Practical Guide*, published by Allyn & Bacon, Boston, MA, ©2001, by Pearson Education)

A look at 50 years of research "on the way teachers teach and learners learn" reveals seven broad principles of good teaching practice (Chickering and Gamson, 1987).

1. Frequent student-faculty contact: Faculty who are concerned about their students and their progress and who are perceived to be easy to talk to, serve to motivate and keep students involved. Things you can do to apply this principle:
- ✓ Attend events sponsored by students.
- ✓ Serve as a mentor or advisor to students.
- ✓ Keep "open" or "drop-in" office hours.

2. The encouragement of cooperation among students: There is a wealth of research indicating that students benefit from the use of small group and peer learning instructional approaches. Things you can do to apply this principle:
- ✓ Have students share in class their interests and backgrounds.
- ✓ Create small groups to work on projects together.
- ✓ Encourage students to study together.

3. Active learning techniques: Students don't learn much by sitting in the classroom listening; they must talk about what they are learning, write about it, relate to it, and apply it to their lives. Things you can do to apply this principle:
- ✓ Give students actual problems or situations to analyze.
- ✓ Use role-playing, simulations or hands-on experiments.
- ✓ Encourage students to challenge ideas brought into class.

4. Prompt feedback: Learning theory research has consistently shown that the quicker the feedback, the greater the learning. Things you can do to apply this principle:
- ✓ Return quizzes and exams by the next class meeting.
- ✓ Return homework within one week.
- ✓ Provide students with detailed comments on their written papers.

5. Emphasize time on task: This principle refers to the amount of actual involvement with the material being studied and applies, obviously, to the way the instructor uses classroom instructional time. Faculty need good time-management skills. Things you can do to apply this principle:
- ✓ Require students who miss classes to make up lost work.
- ✓ Require students to rehearse before making oral presentations.
- ✓ Don't let class breaks stretch out too long.

6. Communicating high expectations: The key here is not to make the course impossibly difficult, but to have goals that can be attained as long as individual learners stretch and work hard, going beyond what they already know. Things you can do to apply this principle:
- ✓ Communicate your expectations orally and in writing at the beginning of the course.
- ✓ Explain the penalties for students who turn work in late.
- ✓ Identify excellent work by students; display exemplars if possible.

7. Respecting diverse talents and ways of learning: Within any classroom there will be students who have latent talents and some with skills and abilities far beyond any that you might imagine. Understanding your students as individuals and showing regard for their unique talents is "likely to

facilitate student growth and development in every sphere – academic, social, personal, and vocational" (Sorcinelli, 1991, p.21). Things you can do to apply this principle:
- ✓ Use diverse teaching approaches.
- ✓ Allow students some choice of readings and assignments.
- ✓ Try to find out students' backgrounds and interests.

Tips for Thriving: Creating an Inclusive Classroom

How do you model an open, accepting attitude within your classroom where students will feel it is safe to engage in give-and-take discussions? Firstly, view students as individuals instead of representatives of separate and distinct groups. Cultivate a climate that is respectful of diverse viewpoints, and don't allow ridicule, defamatory or hurtful remarks. Try to encourage everyone in the class to participate, and be alert to showing favoritism.

2 Today's Undergraduate Students

(Adapted from: Lyons et al, *The Adjunct Professor's Guide to Success*, published by Allyn & Bacon, Boston, MA, ©1999, by Pearson Education)

Total enrollment in all forms of higher education has increased over 65% in the last thirty years. Much of this increase was among part-time students who now comprise over 70% of total college enrollment. The number of "nontraditional" students, typically defined as 25 years of age or older, has been growing more rapidly than the number of "traditional" students, those under 25 years of age. Though there is a great deal of common ground between students of any age, there are some key differences between younger and older students.

Traditional students: Much more than in previous generations, traditional students are the products of dysfunctional families and have had a less effective primary and secondary education. Traditional students have been conditioned by the aftermath of high-profile ethical scandals (such as Watergate), creating a mindset of cynicism and lack of respect for authority figures – including college professors. Students of this generation are quick to proclaim their "rights". Many of today's students perceive professors as service providers, class attendance as a matter of individual choice, and grades as "pay" to which they are entitled for meeting standards they perceive as reasonable.

Nontraditional students: Many older students are attending college after a long lay-off, frequently doubting their ability to succeed. The other time-consuming challenges in their lives – children, work, caring for aging parents – often prevent adequate preparation for class or contribute to frequent absences. While traditional students demand their "rights," many older students won't ask for the smallest extra consideration (e.g., to turn a project in a few days late). Most older students learn best by doing, by applying the theory of the textbook to the rich set of experiences they have accumulated over the years.

Emerging influences: Today, a fourth of all undergraduate students are members of minority groups. Obviously, ethnicity, language, religion, culture, and sexual orientation are each significant issues to which a professor should be sensitive. The successful professor sees these differences as an opportunity rather than a threat to learning.

Tips for Thriving: Be a "Facilitator of Learning"

Be energized by students who "don't get it" rather than judgmental of their shortcomings. View yourself as a "facilitator of learning" rather than a "sage on a stage."

What students want from college professors: While each student subgroup has particular characteristics that affect the dynamics of a college learning environment, students consistently need the following from their college instructors:

- ✓ Consistently communicated expectations of student performance that are reasonable in quantity and quality
- ✓ Sensitivity to the diverse demands on students and reasonable flexibility in accommodating them
- ✓ Effective use of classroom time
- ✓ A classroom environment that includes humor and spontaneity
- ✓ Examinations that address issues properly covered in class and are appropriate to the level of the majority of the students in the class
- ✓ Consistently positive treatment of individual students

The new paradigm of "colleges and universities as service providers to consumer-oriented students" is now firmly entrenched. The successful professor will do well to embrace it.

3 Planning Your Course

(Adapted from Royse, *Teaching Tips for College and University Instructors: A Practical Guide*, published by Allyn & Bacon, Boston, MA, ©2001, by Pearson Education)

Constructing the syllabus: The syllabus should clearly communicate course objectives, assignments, required readings, and grading policies. Think of the syllabus as a stand-alone document. Those students who miss the first or second meeting of a class should be able to learn most of what they need to know about the requirements of the course from reading the syllabus. Start by collecting syllabi from colleagues who have recently taught the course you will be teaching and look for common threads and themes.

Problems to avoid: One mistake commonly made by educators teaching a course for the first time is that they may have rich and intricate visions of how they want students to demonstrate comprehension and synthesis of the material, but they somehow fail to convey this information to those enrolled. Check your syllabus to make sure your expectations have been fully articulated. Be very specific. Avoid vaguely worded instructions:

Instruction	Students may interpret as:
"Write a short paper."	Write a paragraph.
	Write half a page.
	Type a two-page paper.
"Keep a log of your experiences."	Make daily entries.
	Make an entry when the spirit moves me.
	At the end of term, record what I recall.
"Obtain an article from the library."	Any magazine article.
	An article from a professional journal.
	A column from a newsletter.

Tips for Thriving: Visual Quality

Students today are highly visual learners, so you should give special emphasis to the visual quality of the materials you provide to students. Incorporate graphics into your syllabus and other handouts. Color-code your materials so material for different sections of the course are on different colored papers. Such visuals are likely to create a perception among students that you are contemporary.

Teaching Tips for First-time Instructors and Adjunct Professors

4   Your First Class

(Adapted from: Lyons et al, *The Adjunct Professor's Guide to Success*, published by Allyn & Bacon, Boston, MA, ©1999, by Pearson Education)

Success in achieving a great start is almost always directly attributable to the quality and quantity of planning that has been invested by the course professor. If the first meeting of your class is to be successful, you should strive to achieve seven distinct goals.

Create a Positive First Impression: Renowned communications consultant Roger Ailes (1996) claims you have fewer than 10 seconds to create a positive image of yourself. Students are greatly influenced by the visual component; therefore you must look the part of the professional professor. Dress as you would for a professional job interview. Greet each student entering the room. Be approachable and genuine.

Introduce Yourself Effectively: Communicate to students who you are and why you are credible as the teacher of the course. Seek to establish your approachability by "building common ground," such as stating your understanding of students' hectic lifestyles or their common preconceptions toward the subject matter.

Clarify the Goals and Expectations: Make an acetate transparency of each page of the syllabus for display on an overhead projector and using a cover sheet, expose each section as you explain it. Provide clarification and elicit questions.

Conduct an Activity that Introduces Students to Each Other: Students' chances of being able to complete a course effectively is enhanced if each comes to perceive the classmates as a "support network." The small amount of time you invest in an icebreaker will help create a positive classroom atmosphere and pay additional dividends throughout the term.

 Tips for Thriving: Icebreaker

The following activity allows students to get acquainted, exchange opinions, and consider new ideas, values or solutions to problems. It's a great way to promote self-disclosure or an active exchange of viewpoints.

Procedure

1. Give students one or more Post-it™ notes
2. Ask them to write on their note(s) one of the following:
    a. A *value* they hold
    b. An *experience* they have had recently
    c. A *creative idea* or solution to a problem you have posed
    d. A *question* they have about the subject matter of the class
    e. An *opinion* they hold about a topic of your choosing
    f. A *fact* about themselves or the subject matter of the class
3. Ask students to stick the note(s) on their clothing and circulate around the room reading each other's notes.
4. Next, have students mingle once again and negotiate a trade of Post-it™ notes with one another. The trade should be based on a desire to possess a particular value, experience, idea, question, opinion or fact for a short period of time. Set the rule that all trades have to be two-way. Encourage students to make as many trades as they like.
5. Reconvene the class and ask students to share what trades they made and why. (e.g., "I traded for a note that Sally had stating that she has traveled to Eastern Europe. I would really like to travel there because I have ancestors from Hungary and the Ukraine.")

(Adapted from: Silverman, *Active Learning: 101 Strategies to Teach Any Subject*, published by Allyn & Bacon, Boston, MA, ©1996, by Pearson Education).

Learn Students' Names: A student who is regularly addressed by name feels more valued, is invested more effectively in classroom discussion, and will approach the professor with questions and concerns.

Whet Students' Appetite for the Course Material: The textbook adopted for the course is critical to your success. Your first meeting should include a review of its approach, features, and sequencing. Explain to students what percentage of class tests will be derived from material from the textbook.

Reassure Students of the Value of the Course: At the close of your first meeting reassure students that the course will be a valuable learning experience and a wise investment of their time. Review the reasons why the course is a good investment: important and relevant content, interesting classmates, and a dynamic classroom environment.

5   Strategies for Teaching and Learning

(Adapted from: Silverman, *Active Learning: 101 Strategies to Teach Any Subject,* published by Allyn & Bacon, Boston, MA, © 1996, by Pearson Education)

Getting participation through active learning: To learn something well, it helps to hear it, see it, ask questions about it, and discuss it with others. What makes learning "active"? When learning is active, students do most of the work: they use their brains to study ideas, solve problems, and apply what they learn. Active learning is fast-paced, fun, supportive, and personally engaging. Active learning cannot occur without student participation, so there are various ways to structure discussion and obtain responses from students at any time during a class. Here are ten methods to get participation at any time:

1. **Open discussion**. Ask a question and open it up to the entire class without further structuring.
2. **Response cards**. Pass out index cards and request anonymous answers to your questions.
3. **Polling**. Design a short survey that is filled out and tallied on the spot.
4. **Subgroup discussion**. Break students into subgroups of three or more to share and record information.
5. **Learning partners**. Have students work on tasks with the student sitting next to them.
6. **Whips**. Go around the group and obtain short responses to key questions – invite students to pass if they wish.
7. **Panels**. Invite a small number of students to present their views in front of the class.
8. **Fishbowl**. Ask a portion of the class to form a discussion circle and have the remaining students form a listening circle around them. Bring new groups into the inner circle to continue the discussion.
9. **Games**. Use a fun exercise or quiz game to elicit students' ideas, knowledge, or skill.
10. **Calling on the next speaker**. Ask students to raise their hands when they want to share their views and ask the current speaker to choose the next speaker.

(Adapted from Royse, *Teaching Tips for College and University Instructors: A Practical Guide,* published by Allyn & Bacon, Boston, MA, ©2001, by Pearson Education)

Team learning: The essential features of this small group learning approach, developed originally for use in large college classrooms are (1) relatively permanent heterogeneous task groups; (2) grading based on a combination of individual performance, group performance, and peer evaluation; (3) organization of the course so that the majority of class time is spent on small group activities; (4) a six-step instructional process similar to the following model:

1. Individual study of material outside of the class is assigned.
2. Individual testing is used (multiple choice questions over homework at the beginning of class)
3. Groups discuss their answers and then are given a group test of the same items. They then get immediate feedback (answers).
4. Groups may prepare written appeals of items.

5. Feedback is given from instructor.
6. An application-oriented activity is assigned (e.g. a problem to be solved requiring input from all group members).

If you plan to use team learning in your class, inform students at the beginning of the course of your intentions to do so and explain the benefits of small group learning. Foster group cohesion by sitting groups together and letting them choose "identities" such as a team name or slogan. You will need to structure and supervise the groups and ensure that the projects build on newly acquired learning. Make the projects realistic and interesting and ensure that they are adequately structured so that each member's contribution is 25 percent. Students should be given criteria by which they can assess and evaluate the contributions of their peers on a project-by-project basis (Michaelsen, 1994).

Tips for Thriving: Active Learning and Lecturing

Lecturing is one of the most time-honored teaching methods, but does it have a place in an active learning environment? There are times when lecturing can be effective. Think about the following when planning a lecture:

Build Interest: Capture your students' attention by leading off with an anecdote or cartoon.
Maximize Understanding and Retention: Use brief handouts and demonstrations as a visual backup to enable your students to see as well as hear.
Involve Students during the Lecture: Interrupt the lecture occasionally to challenge students to answer spot quiz questions.
Reinforce the Lecture: Give students a self-scoring review test at the end of the lecture.

6   Grading and Assessment Techniques

(Adapted from Wankat, *The Effective, Efficient Professor: Teaching, Scholarship and Service*, published by Allyn & Bacon, Boston, MA, ©2002, by Pearson Education)

Philosophy of grading: Develop your own philosophy of grading by picturing in your mind the performance of typical A students, B students and so on. Try different grading methods until you find one that fits your philosophy and is reasonably fair. Always look closely at students on grade borders – take into account personal factors if the group is small. Be consistent with or slightly more generous than the procedure outlined in your syllabus.

Criterion grading: Professor Philip Wankat writes: "I currently use a form of criterion grading for my sophomore and junior courses. I list the scores in the syllabus that will guarantee the students As, Bs and so forth. For example, a score of 85 to 100 guarantees an A; 75 to 85, a B; 65 to 75, a C; and 55 to 65, a D. If half the class gets above 85% they all get an A. This reduces competition and allows students to work together and help each other. The standard grade gives students something to aim for and tells them exactly what their grade is at any time. For students whose net scores are close to the borders at the end of the course, I look at other factors before deciding a final grade such as attendance."

Tips for Thriving: Result Feedback

As stated earlier, feedback on results is the most effective of motivating factors. Anxious students are especially hungry for positive feedback. You can quickly and easily provide it by simply writing "Great job!" on the answer sheets or tests. For students who didn't perform well, a brief note such as "I'd love to talk with you at the end of class" can be especially reassuring. The key is to be proactive and maintain high standards, while requiring students to retain ownership of their success.

7 Using Technology

(Adapted from: Sanders, *Creating Learning-Centered Courses for the World Wide Web*, published by Allyn & Bacon, Boston, MA, ©2001, by Pearson Education)

The Web as a source of teaching and learning has generated a great deal of excitement and hyperbole. The Web is neither a panacea nor a demon, but it can be a valuable tool. Among the many misunderstandings about the use of Web pages for teaching and learning is a view that such efforts must encompass an entire course. Like any other tool in a course (e.g. lectures, discussions, films, or field trips) online material can be incorporated to enhance the learning experience.

The best way to start using the Web in a course is with small steps. Developing a single lesson or assignment, a syllabus, or a few well-chosen links makes more sense than trying to develop a whole course without sufficient support or experience. Testing Web materials with a class that regularly meets face-to-face helps a faculty member gauge how well a lesson using the Web works. Making adjustments within the context of a traditional class helps fine-tune Web lessons that may be offered in distance education without face-to-face interaction.

 Tips for Thriving: Using Videos

Generally a videotape should not exceed half and hour in length. Always preview a video before showing it to ensure the content, language, and complexity are appropriate for your students. Include major videos on your syllabus to encourage attendance and integrate them into the context of the course. Plan to evaluate students' retention of the concepts on exams or through reports. Avoid reinforcing the common student perception that watching a video is a time-filler.

By beginning with good practices in learning, we ask not how the new technology can help us do a better job of getting students to learn, but rather we ask how good pedagogy be better implemented with the new technology.

8 Managing Problem Situations

(Adapted from Wankat, *The Effective, Efficient Professor: Teaching, Scholarship and Service*, published by Allyn & Bacon, Boston, MA, ©2002, by Pearson Education)

Cheating: Cheating is one behavior that should not be tolerated. Tolerating cheating tends to make it worse. Prevention of cheating is much more effective than trying to cure it once it has occurred. A professor can prevent cheating by:

- Creating rapport with students
- Gaining a reputation for giving fair tests
- Giving clear instructions and guidelines before, during, and after tests
- Educating students on the ethics of plagiarism
- Requiring periodic progress reports and outlines before a paper is due

Try to develop exams that are perceived as fair and secure by students. Often, the accusation that certain questions were tricky is valid as it relates to ambiguous language and trivial material. Ask your mentor or an experienced instructor to closely review the final draft of your first few exams for these factors.

Tips for Thriving: Discipline

One effective method for dealing with some discipline problems is to ask the class for feedback (Angelo & Cross, 1993) In a one-minute quiz, ask the students, "What can I do to help you learn?" Collate the responses and present them to the class. If behavior such as excessive talking appears in some responses (e.g. "Tell people to shut up") this gives you the backing to ask students to be quiet. Use of properly channeled peer pressure is often effective in controlling undesired behavior

(Adapted from Royse, *Teaching Tips for College and University Instructors: A Practical Guide*, published by Allyn & Bacon, Boston, MA, ©2001, by Pearson Education)

Unmotivated Students: There are numerous reasons why students may not be motivated. The "required course" scenario is a likely explanation – although politics in colonial America is your life's work, it is safe to assume that not everyone will share your enthusiasm. There are also personal reasons such as a death of a loved one or depression. Whenever you detect a pattern that you assume to be due to lack of motivation (e.g. missing classes, not handing assignments in on time, non-participation in class), arrange a time to have the student meet with you outside the classroom. Candidly express your concerns and then listen.

Motivating students is part of the faculty members' job. To increase motivation professors should: show enthusiasm for the topic; use various media and methods to present material; use humor in the classroom; employ activities that encourage active learning; and give frequent, positive feedback.

(Adapted from Baiocco/Waters, *Successful College Teaching*, published by Allyn & Bacon, Boston, MA, ©1998, by Pearson Education)

Credibility Problems. If you are an inexperienced instructor you may have problems with students not taking you seriously. At the first class meeting articulate clear rules of classroom decorum and comport yourself with dignity and respect for students. Try to exude that you are in charge and are the "authority" and avoid trying to pose as the students' friend.

9   Surviving When You're Not Prepared

(Adapted from: Lyons et al, *The Adjunct Professor's Guide to Success*, published by Allyn & Bacon, Boston, MA, ©1999, by Pearson Education)

Despite your thorough course planning, your concern for students, and commitment to the institution, situations will arise – illness, family emergencies – that prevent you from being fully prepared for every class meeting. Most students will excuse one flawed performance during a term, but try to develop contingency plans you can employ on short notice. These might include:

- Recruiting a guest speaker from your circle of colleagues to deliver a presentation that might interest your students.
- Conducting a carousel brainstorming activity, in which a course issue is examined from several perspectives. Divide the students in to groups to identify facts appropriate to each perspective. For example, you might want to do a SWOT analysis (Strengths, Weaknesses, Opportunities, Threats) on a particular organization or public figure.
- Dividing the class into groups of three or four and asking them to develop several questions that would be appropriate for inclusion on your next exam.
- Identify a video at your local rental store that embellishes material from the course.
- Assign students roles (e.g. press, governmental figures, etc.), and conduct a focused analysis of a late-breaking news story related to your course.
- Divide students into groups to work on an assigned course project or upcoming exam.
- As a last resort, admit your inability to prepare a class and allow students input into formulating a strategy for best utilizing class time.

In each case, the key is to shift the initial attention away from yourself (to permit you to gather your thoughts) and onto an activity that engages students in a new and significant way.

10   Improving Your Performance

(Adapted from: Lyons et al, *The Adjunct Professor's Guide to Success*, published by Allyn & Bacon, Boston, MA, ©1999, by Pearson Education)

The instructor who regularly engages in systematic self-evaluation will unquestionably derive greater reward from the formal methods of evaluation commonly employed by colleges and universities. One method for providing structure to an ongoing system of self-evaluation is to keep a journal of reflections on your teaching experiences. Regularly invest 15 or 20 introspective minutes following each class meeting to focus especially on the strategies and events in class that you feel could be improved. Committing your thoughts and emotions enables you to develop more effective habits, build confidence in your teaching performance, and make more effective comparisons later. The following questions will help guide self-assessment:

How do I typically begin the class?
Where/How do I position myself in the class?
How do I move in the classroom?
Where are my eyes usually focused?
Do I facilitate students' visual processing of course material?
Do I change the speed, volume, energy, and tone of my voice?
How do I ask questions of students?
How often, and when, do I smile or laugh in class?
How do I react when students are inattentive?
How do I react when students disagree or challenge what I say?
How do I typically end a class?

 Tips for Thriving: Video-Recording Your Class

In recent years a wide range if professionals have markedly improved their job performance by employing video recorders in their preparation efforts. As an instructor, an effective method might be to ask your mentor or another colleague to tape a 10 to 15 minute mini-lesson then to debrief it using the assessment questions above. Critiquing a videotaped session provides objectivity and is therefore more likely to effect change. Involving a colleague as an informal coach will enable you to gain from their experience and perspective and will reduce the chances of your engaging in self-deprecation.

References

Ailes, R. (1996) *You are the message: Getting what you want by being who you are.* New York: Doubleday.
Chickering, A.W., & Gamson, Z.F. (1987) Seven principles for good practice in undergraduate education. AAHE Bulletin, 39, 3-7.
Michaelson, L.K. (1994). Team Learning: Making a case for the small-group option. In K.W. Prichard & R.M. Sawyer (Eds.), *Handbook of college teaching.* Westport, CT: Greenwood Press.
Sorcinelli, M.D. (1991). Research findings on the seven principles. In A.W. Chickering & Z. Gamson (eds.), *Applying the seven principles of good practice in undergraduate education.* New Directions for Teaching and Learning #47. San Francisco: Jossey-Bass.